P9-CLE-292

Table of Contents

iii

Table of Contents

Issues'88

A Platform for America
Domestic Policy Planks

Edited by **Mark B. Liedl**

Contributors

Stuart M. Butler   Edmund F. Haislmaier

John E. Buttarazzi   Edward L. Hudgins

Milton R. Copulos   Stephen Moore

Peter J. Ferrara   William Peterson

Eileen M. Gardner   Robert Rector

James L. Gattuso   Melanie S. Tammen

The Heritage Foundation

Mark B. Liedl is a Washington political and public policy analyst. He formerly served as Research Director of the National Republican Senatorial Committee. Mr. Liedl holds a B.A. in Political Science from the University of Minnesota and is completing his graduate studies in jurisprudence at Georgetown University.

———

Acknowledgements

To Tess Samuel, Don Hall, Sue Matteson, and Richard Odermatt for their editorial and production assistance.

Library of Congress Cataloging in Publication Number 88-80277.

ISBN 0-89195-043-5

Copyright 1988 by The Heritage Foundation.

Foreword

America is at a crossroads. For the first time in two decades, an incumbent president will not be running for re-election. This makes 1988 a year of enormous debate. It is a debate that turns on the distinction between those who believe Washington has all the answers and those who believe Washington should listen to the American people. Listening to the people, however, is not something that Washington does well. There long has been a disjunction between the capital and the vast American heartland. Were Washington to listen, it would hear Americans asking for the power to control their own destinies — the liberty to create their own opportunities, and the freedom to make their own decisions at the state, local, and family levels. Washington would hear that Americans want a strong and secure nation that preserves peace by protecting freedom. And they want no U-turn back to the economic and social excesses of the 1970s and government policies that fail to reflect traditional American values.

It is to force Washington to listen more closely to the American public and to translate what it hears into specific policies that The Free Congress Research and Education Foundation and The Heritage Foundation offer *Issues '88*, with its platform of 238 planks for a stronger and healthier America based on sound conservative principles. Domestic and foreign and defense issues are addressed by the staff of The Heritage Foundation in Volume One and Volume Two, respectively; social policy reforms appear in Volume Three, produced by the staff of The Free Congress Research and Education Foundation.

More than a policy document, *Issues '88* is a blueprint for mobilizing a broad coalition of Americans. This coalition defies traditional partisan labels. It consists of Americans of all parties, sectors, and geographic areas who would build on the accomplishments of the Reagan years rather than retreat to the failed policies of earlier periods. And these Americans, on a broad range of attitudes and policies, are in the majority. In short, this is a blueprint for making America number one again.

Polling data reveal, for instance, that a majority of Americans prefers that government let "each person get ahead on his own" to government attempts to guarantee that "each person has a job and a good standard of living." A majority believes that government does too many things that should be left to private individuals or businesses and that "government creates more problems than it solves," although the majority also wants an activist program for governing. This document supplies such a program. The conservative majority believes in the power and importance of the traditional family, while the liberal minority regards the family simply as one of any number of idiosyncratic lifestyles and of no special importance. The majority credits hard work by the American family as the foundation of the nation's economic growth.

The conservative majority, polls confirm, believes that softness threatens freedom, while the liberal minority talks and acts as if American strength threatens peace. The majority believes freedom has primacy over peace, that the best way to avoid war is to be militarily prepared to fight one, and that the U.S. occupies a distinctly higher moral plane than the USSR. The majority mistrusts Moscow, believes the Soviets are an expansionist empire, and applauds Winston Churchill's advice that:

> ...it's no use arguing with a communist. It's no use trying to convert a communist, or persuade him....You can only deal with them...by having superior force on your side....If you wish for peace, it is absolutely necessary that you should be the stronger.

Washington is out of step with this American majority. The values and aspirations of the American people are ignored in most key policies pursued by the federal government. While Americans seek conservative solutions to critical problems, Washington clings to the special interest politics of the past. While Americans ask for a strong and fiscally secure America, Washington offers cuts in national defense and higher taxes.

Issues '88 builds on the concerns and desires of America's conservative majority. *Issues '88* offers domestic policies which empower the individual rather than government. It presents policies for a strong and prudent national defense and a foreign policy which demand freedom and judges the Soviets and their colonies by ac-

ix

tions not words. And it proposes social policy solutions which challenge the responsibilities of individuals and restore the traditional power of the family.

The lessons of history teach that mere knowledge of truth is insufficient. As such, *Issues '88* discusses the strategies and tactics required to turn the proposed planks into solid policy. It identifies the political forces obstructing the majority's will, and proposes action for removing these obstacles. *Issues '88* outlines coalition and constituent-building strategies to accomplish specific policy goals.

A quarter of a century has passed since an American president has faced the constitutional prohibition of three terms in office. The decades since then have witnessed a tremendous explosion in the size and scope of the federal government, an assault on traditional values, turmoil at home, and setbacks for America abroad. In 1981, Ronald Reagan assumed command of a nation in decline. Yet as he enters his eighth year, America is stronger and freer, but there is much more to be done. Most of the steps forward that have been taken are not permanent and could easily be undone. That is why permanent constituencies must be identified to support real reforms.

America cannot afford to step back. It must not turn to the past to meet the challenges of the future. Ronald Reagan began to turn America away from the failures of the 1970s. The task now is to carry America into the opportunities of the 1990s. We hope that *Issues '88* will help lead the way.

Edwin J. Feulner, Jr.
President
The Heritage Foundation

Paul M. Weyrich
President
The Free Congress
     Research and
     Education Foundation

Washington, D.C.
March 1988

Domestic Policy Planks

Plank 1. Pass a constitutional balanced budget amendment containing a tax limitation clause.

Plank 2. Give the President a line-item veto.

Plank 3. Adopt a two-year budget cycle.

Plank 4. Abolish subsidies to businesses from such agencies as Urban Development Action Grants, the Export-Import Bank, and the Small Business Administration.

Plank 5. Contract out federal services.

Plank 6. Merge federal aid programs to the states into a single Fiscal Capacity Grant and combine it with a tax cut.

Plank 7. Encourage cities and states to seek private sector financing for infrastructure improvements.

Plank 8. Privatize federal assets and programs.

Plank 9. Limit federal non-defense spending to 15 percent of GNP by 1992.

Plank 10. Adopt Grace Commission Reforms.

Plank 11. Reform the military retirement system.

Plank 12. Block tax increases for deficit reduction.

Plank 13. Establish a commission to review all entitlements programs.

Plank 14. Create a Commission on Economic Growth to emphasize growth-oriented policies.

Plank 15. Reduce the capital gains tax rate from 28 percent to 15 percent.

Plank 16. Reduce taxes which discourage savings by expanding IRAs and insuring Family Investment Plans.

Plank 17. Increase personal exemptions and fund this by repealing the federal deduction for state and local taxes.

Plank 18. Remove barriers to interstate banking.

Plank 19. Repeal the Glass-Steagall Act, which separates commercial and investment banking.

Plank 20. Resist regulations hindering corporate takeovers.

Plank 21. Sell federal direct loan originations to private buyers.

Plank 22. Reinsure government loan guarantees with private insurance.

Plank 23. Reaffirm the right of the employee to join or not join labor unions.

Plank 24. Ban diversion of union dues to political or ideological purposes if employees object.

Plank 25. Empower federal authorities to prosecute violence or the threat of violence in labor disputes.

Plank 26. Restore flexibility to public sector pay.

Plank 27. Reject gender-based pay scales.

Plank 28. Promote employment opportunities by reforming minimum wage laws.

Plank 29. Expand Americans' right to work at home.

Plank 30. Cut marginal tax rates to stimulate risk-taking and small business ventures.

Plank 31. Repeal the Corporate Average Fuel Economy standards on U.S. auto companies.

Plank 32. Decontrol natural gas prices fully.

Plank 33. Shift the emphasis of safety regulation from safety standards based on specific equipment to standards based on results.

Plank 34. Require "Job and Competitiveness Impact Statements" for new government rules and regulations.

Plank 35. Modify the merger restrictions in Section 7 of the Clayton Act.

Plank 36. Prohibit anti-merger lawsuits by competitors.

Plank 37. Abolish automatic treble damages rules.

Plank 38. Set reasonable standards for product liability suits.

Plank 39. Reform unemployment insurance to reward displaced workers who find new jobs quickly.

Plank 40. Tighten the Freedom of Information Act to ensure the confidentiality of U.S. trade secrets.

Plank 41. Strengthen international agreements affecting "intellectual property rights."

Plank 42. Require the Congressional Budget Office to issue regular statistics on the costs of U.S. trade protectionism to consumers and businesses.

Plank 43. Remove barriers to the development and export of natural gas from Alaska's North Slope.

Plank 44. Allow the export of raw timber harvested on public lands.

Plank 45. Change cargo preference rules that raise the prices of U.S. agricultural exports.

Plank 46. Remove "voluntary" quota restrictions and dismantle U.S.-enforced cartels that restrict supplies of goods and raw materials in the U.S.

Plank 47. Participate in the Uruguay Round of the General Agreement on Tariffs and Trade and reject legislation violating this agreement.

Plank 48. Begin negotiations to phase out all agricultural trade barriers and subsidies.

Plank 49. Create Free Trade Areas with countries that seek totally open markets.

Plank 50. Promote growth-oriented economic policies in developing countries by linking U.S. aid to deregulation, tax reform, and privatization.

Plank 51. Promote debt-for-equity swaps to ease Third World debt and spur reforms.

Plank 52. Promote employee stock ownership plans in LDCs as a means to privatize state-owned industries and widen capital ownership.

Plank 53. Oppose new U.S. contributions to the International Monetary Fund, the World Bank, Inter-American Development Bank, and other multinational banks that encourage destructive economic policies.

Plank 54. Strengthen the Caribbean Basin Initiative by eliminating existing trade restrictions.

Plank 55. Oppose the admission of the Soviet Union to the International Monetary Fund (IMF), the World Bank, and the General Agreement on Tariffs and Trade (GATT).

Plank 56. Defend airline deregulation and extend market mechanisms to airports and airways.

Plank 57. Further deregulate trucking rates and routes at the state and federal levels.

Plank 58. Re-examine the "Jones Act."

Plank 59. Privatize the air traffic control system.

Plank 60. Privatize Amtrak's northeast corridor.

Plank 61. End federal funding of the interstate highway system.

Plank 62. End federal restrictions on state highway spending.

Plank 63. Replace the current mass transit grant structure with a single Urban Transit Block Grant.

Plank 64. Create a Space Enterprise Zone.

Plank 65. End subsidies to wealthy farmers.

Plank 66. Decouple farm subsidies from production decisions.

Plank 67. Abolish farm marketing orders.

Plank 68. Encourage agriculture "options" in place of price supports.

Plank 69. Create a Wilderness Board to administer wilderness areas.

Plank 70. End Forest Service destruction of forests.

Plank 71. Increase state and local control of hazardous waste policy.

Plank 72. Use market mechanisms, such as a production rights market, to achieve pollution goals.

Plank 73. Review Environmental Protection Agency grant incentives to encourage private sector financing and operation of wastewater plants.

Plank 74. Reform land use policy.

Plank 75. Reform resource tax policy.

Plank 76. Decentralize mine waste regulation.

Plank 77. Reduce mineral vulnerability.

Plank 78. Change health insurance regulations and tax treatment to reduce the cost of individual and family policies.

Plank 79. Require individuals to purchase catastrophic health insurance or pre-paid health plans for themselves and their families.

Plank 80. Reform medigap insurance rules to cover all non-Medicare reimbursed charges over $2,000 instead of current "first dollar" coverage.

Plank 81. Shift most health care tax breaks from the corporate to the individual tax code to encourage individuals to purchase insurance and medical services directly.

Plank 82. Make corporate plans for retiree health insurance tax deductible.

Plank 83. Exempt health care tax deductions for needy relatives from the current dependent support test.

Plank 84. Support Health Care Savings Accounts.

Plank 85. Convert Medicare, Medicaid, and veteran's health care programs to voucher systems.

Plank 86. Contract for private sector veteran's care.

Plank 87. Contract with corporations to provide Medicare services for their retirees.

Plank 88. Abolish local economic development programs.

Plank 89. Abolish the Department of Housing and Urban Development.

Plank 90. Replace low income housing assistance with vouchers.

Plank 91. Privatize the Federal Housing and Mortgage Agencies.

Plank 92. Offer federal housing aid only to cities that do not control rents.

Plank 93. Amend the 1963 Community Mental Health Centers Act to stop mentally ill Americans from being turned onto the streets.

Plank 94. Decentralize decision making to states and localities and give federal grants only to poorer states.

Plank 95. Cut federal contributions to states with high welfare benefits.

Plank 96. Enact authentic workfare legislation.

Plank 97. Enforce financial responsibilities of parents.

Plank 98. Use vouchers to empower welfare recipients and reduce dependency on the "poverty industry."

Plank 99. Reduce restrictions on community organizations providing services to the poor.

Plank 100. Reduce welfare benefits to individuals with income above the poverty line; where appropriate, provide a corresponding income tax deduction to offset the reduction in welfare benefits.

Plank 101. Give states the option to tailor Aid to Families with Dependent Children payment levels.

Plank 102. Guarantee Social Security Benefits.

Plank 103. Require an annual Social Security "statement of account."

Plank 104. Create a "Super IRA."

Plank 105. Foster private pensions and enhance their transferability.

Plank 106. Reduce payroll tax rates.

Plank 107. Make education vouchers available for low income Americans.

Plank 108. Reduce regulatory impediments to private schools serving low income families.

Plank 109. Increase law enforcement in the inner-city.

Plank 110. Adopt a crime victims' Bill of Rights.

Plank 111. Support neighborhood crime prevention programs.

Plank 112. Encourage municipalities to contract with neighborhood groups to provide municipal services.

Plank 113. Reduce barriers to minority businesses rather than making them dependent on set-aside programs.

Introduction

by Stuart M. Butler

A Conservative Platform on domestic policy issues differs from a party manifesto because it focuses not on a set of often disjointed policies designed to win a majority of electoral votes, but instead represents the policies associated with a distinct philosophy of government and a clear-headed view of human nature. Yet in keeping with traditional party platforms, it is a practical document, designed to widen the appeal of American conservatism by reaching out to new constituencies without compromising principle, and by looking forward, yet remembering the hard-learned lessons of the past.

This Conservative Platform rests on key principles wrought from experience as much as from philosophy. Among these principles is the notion that a civilized, caring, and tolerant society can only continue to function

Stuart M. Butler is Director of Domestic Policy Studies at The Heritage Foundation

1

if basic values, such as family and social responsibilities, and the liberty of the individual to choose how to live his or her own life, are respected, promoted, and protected by government. Another principle, amply supported by experience, is that a process of free exchange of goods and services, known as the free market, is not only more likely than a regulated economy to enhance general prosperity, but also more likely to discover products and services to serve poor as well as affluent citizens.

An equally important principle concerns the nature of government. Remembering Lord Acton's famous dictum that "power tends to corrupt," conservatives are reluctant to relinquish power to government — even a government composed of conservatives. The record of 200 years of American government warns conservatives that even the most attractive program or responsible agency tends soon to come under the control of narrow interests who use it to reward themselves. And conservatives recognize that pluralism and localism are the lifeblood of government, just as they are of American society.

In keeping with their distrust of government, conservatives are more inclined than liberals to trust the innate good sense of ordinary people and to believe that such Americans are more likely than government to protect their own interests.

Conservatives trust the people. This is why conservatives support ideas like education vouchers, which let poor parents, rather than school officials, decide where their children shall go to school. It is why conservatives call for freer markets and private enterprise in less developed countries as a means of fostering growth, rather than accepting the fashionable liberal view that only multinational lending agencies and central government planning can create wealth. It is why conservatives are willing to sit down with poor Americans and ask them what works in welfare and what does not, rather than analyzing the poor as data. And it is also why conservatives demand of poor people the same degree of family personal responsibility as they would of any other group of Americans.

The 113 planks of this volume lay out a plan of action based on these principles. It is a plan to bring greater prosperity to Americans, while addressing the needs of less fortunate citizens in a humane, just, and effective way. The planks cover such areas as the proper role and scale of the federal government, the best tax and monetary framework to assure strong and stable economic growth, the issue of U.S. competitiveness in world markets, the future of American agriculture, the environment, and the health and welfare of poorer Americans.

Several central themes run through this document. One is the idea of genuine consumerism. Unlike the liberal

3

view of consumerism, which invariably results in consumers finding their choices restricted and more expensive, the conservative notion of consumerism involves giving Americans the greatest possible range of choices in the most competitive economic framework. Thus Plank 18 would remove remaining barriers to interstate banking, Planks 42 through 46 would reduce protectionism, which limits the freedom of consumers, and Plank 90 would provide low-income families with housing vouchers, so that they could choose where they wish to live, rather than being assigned housing by bureaucrats.

Another key theme recognizes the political dynamics which make it impossible for Congress either to control spending or to establish clear priorities for federal action. Thus Plank 1 calls for a constitutional amendment to balance the budget and limit spending, to place constraints on Congress. Similarly, Plank 2 would give the President a line-item veto to restore an important constitutional check in the congressional budget process. And recognizing the reluctance of lawmakers to tackle such politically sensitive issues as entitlement programs, Plank 13 would establish a commission to review all entitlement programs for the middle class as well as those serving the poor.

Privatization is another central theme. In some cases this involves transferring commercial activities to the private sector where they belong, and where private-sector incentives will lead to greater efficiency and better service to the consumer. Thus Plank 60 calls for the sale to employees of Amtrak's northeast corridor, and Planks 8 and 21 urge the sale of the federal government's loan portfolio to the private sector.

In other cases, privatization represents an innovative strategy to pursue policy objectives shared by most liberals and conservatives, breaking a political deadlock. For instance, Plank 69 calls for the creation of a Wilderness Board, operated by environmental organizations, to manage sensitive wilderness areas. By changing the ownership of these public lands, the Board would create better management incentives. In addition, Plank 72 calls for a "production rights market," using market mechanisms to bring pollution down to acceptable levels at the smallest cost in lost economic output and jobs.

The privatization theme is also linked with the aim of empowering consumers and trusting ordinary Americans. Hence Plank 98 would use vouchers to enable the poor to make real choices in such areas as education and welfare services, rather than being forced to accept services offered by the "poverty industry" of professional welfare providers. Similarly, fostering the contracting out to neighborhood groups of many municipal services, urged in Plank 99, would enable poor Americans to assume a greater role in providing services. And Planks 107 to 108's call for reduced impediments to minority private schools serving the poor would give a welcome boost to local schools that have succeeded against all the odds.

Several of the planks are based on the theme, supported strongly by recent experience, that incentives are critical for economic dynamism. Hence Plank 15 would reduce capital gains taxes to spur innovative investment and, incidentally, boost tax revenues, while Plank 16 calls for the institution of "Family Investment Plans," designed to encourage the small investor by shielding him from some taxes.

A major theme running throughout the platform is the proper role of the federal government. Thus several planks seek to restructure government activities or to breathe new life into federalism. Some planks call for the ending of a program at the federal level, or its transfer to the states. Thus Plank 4 urges the termination of several programs, such as the Export-Import Bank, which merely subsidize private firms. Plank 62 calls for ending federal restrictions on state highway spending and Plank 6 would overhaul federal grants to states, replacing the current inefficient scattershot approach with a streamlined and targeted "Fiscal Capacity Grant" designed to help only those states who do not have the economic resources to provide for citizen needs.

Other planks in the federalism vein would tap the creative juices of states. Thus Plank 112 would encourage states and localities to contract with neighborhood groups to provide municipal services. States have uséd these mechanisms to experiment with creative ways to provide health insurance coverage to the indigent. Even more important, Plank 94 calls for the systematic use of "waivers" in welfare policy, under which states would be permitted to reorganize existing welfare programs, subject to federal approval, to experiment with innovative strategies to tackle the persistent problems of poverty and welfare dependency.

$$* \quad * \quad *$$

This platform is not merely a wish list. It recognizes that reaching political goals requires a political strategy. It also appreciates that to build the political momentum for change, new coalitions must be forged to widen the appeal of conservative ideas. Building such coalitions is critical to implementing the planks.

Coalition building is particularly important in changing the debate over welfare. Well-constructed conservative proposals in the past have failed to be enacted because little was done to win support for them among the group of Americans with the most to gain — the poor. The dramatic success of conservatives in gaining the vigorous backing of inner city public housing tenants for proposals to privatize public housing is a dramatic lesson of what can be done through coalition building. By working with tenants and using their suggestions to refine the proposal, a remarkable coalition of conservative lawmakers and poor, primarily black, Americans forced liberals in Congress to accept self-management and tenant purchases in public housing.

This platform proposes similar coalition building to achieve other goals. For instance, the stalled momentum for education vouchers could be given a jump-start by forging a coalition with inner city parents who are frustrated with the public schools, and inner city private schools which cater to poorer students. Thus instead of vouchers being seen as a device to allow middle-class Americans to escape the public schools, they would become a mechanism to empower the poor.

This platform takes a similar approach toward the environment. The proposed planks and the strategy associated with them seek to build alliances with moderate environmentalists who are concerned that bureaucratic government management of the environment is threatening wildlife, forests and rangelands. By proposing market based strategies, as privatization, involving a crucial management role for responsible environmentalists, conservatives have the opportunity to win over groups that recently have been some of their strongest opponents.

In conjunction with coalition building in support of planks, it is also important to divide the alliances now blocking conservative reforms. A key target: those politicians or middle class groups who are vocal in their support of programs to aid the poor, yet derive far more benefits from these programs than do the poor themselves, or who in many instances support programs that actually harm the poor. Thus this platform proposes strategies that would attack many "advocates" for the homeless, who wish only to force money from Washington yet avoid local action that actually would help the homeless. Similarly, as part of the consumerist approach, the platform proposes a strategy to fight protectionism that would focus on the consumer costs of blocking imports, and the current high incomes of many workers now seeking protection compared with the incomes of other Americans who would be forced to pay higher prices.

This conservative platform is a document designed to do far more than simply provide a broad philosophical framework or a policy wish list. Its planks reflect a practical set of action plans based on fundamental principles blended with political realism. And its message is not one merely confined to those who call themselves conservatives. It is for all Americans.

9

Chapter One

Federal Spending

Recent congressional efforts to cut the federal deficit underlie the need for fundamental budget reform. A serious effort to get federal spending under control is impossible with the current dynamics of the spending process. Today's huge federal deficits are not the result of low taxes, but of a continually growing public sector which wastes taxpayers' money and threatens economic growth. Since the tax cut of 1981, in fact, federal revenues have increased 50 percent. The problem is that spending has grown even faster — up 54 percent.

To eliminate the federal deficit, to maintain a strong national defense, and to meet the needs of all Americans, Congress must cut its spending drastically. First, congressional discipline must be restored through such spending constraints as the line-item veto and balanced budget amendment. Second, the dynamics of federal spending which fuel the pro-spending lobbies must be altered through innovative alternatives to well-meaning but ineffectual programs. Privatization offers one such approach. Third, spending choices should be made as much as possible at state and local levels rather than by bureaucrats and politicians in Washington.

——— The Budget Process ———

Plank 1. Pass a constitutional balanced budget amendment containing a tax limitation clause.

The size of the national debt has exploded over the last ten years. It took the nation over 200 years to amass a debt of $1 trillion; but, thanks to the triple digit annual budget deficits of the 1980s, it took just six years to amass the nation's second trillion dollars of debt. By 1991 the national debt will exceed $3 trillion — triple its 1980 level.

Every attempt by Congress and the President to balance the budget through their own devices has failed; budget summits produce temporary, hollow victories and the Gramm-Rudman-Hollings balanced budget law is routinely ignored. Congress freely violates its self-imposed budget laws when it is convenient to do so.

But Congress will not be able to disobey the Constitution; an enforceable balanced budget amendment will restrain federal spending and permanently eliminate federal red ink. There are very few issues that command as much support as the balanced budget amendment. A 1987 *New York Times* poll found that over 80 percent of Americans endorse the idea.

Plank 2. Give the President a line-item veto.

Nearly every President since Abraham Lincoln has requested a line-item veto to control federal spending. Such a device would allow the President to veto specific budget items in a spending bill while approving the remainder of the bill.

Empowering the Chief Executive with line-item veto authority would restore some of the Executive Branch's traditional authority over the budget process that has been usurped by Congress. For instance, every President between George Washington and Richard Nixon had the power to "impound" funds — to refuse to spend unnecessary appropriations. Presidents often used this to slice unnecessary spending from the budget. In 1974 the power was rescinded; the weakened presidential role in budget matters has coincided directly with the burgeoning of the federal deficit.

Congress's recent practice of packaging the entire budget into a single bill has been criticized universally and makes a strong case for a line-item veto. In December 1987, for instance, the President was confronted with a $604 billion budget bill, that was 2,100 pages. The President was given the choice that is no choice: sign the bill or shut down the government. A line-item veto would have allowed the President to cut billions of dollars from this budget and would have discouraged irresponsible budget packaging in the first place.

Plank 3. Adopt a two-year budget cycle.

Congress spends nearly the entire year on the budget, and still it rarely completes its budget business before the start of the fiscal year. This often necessitates the passage of eleventh hour Continuing Resolutions, which contain billions of dollars of pork barrel spending items.

To avoid this, Congress should adopt a two-year budget system. This would bind Congress to its deficit reduction promises. Typically, Congress passes budgets with ambitious spending cuts in the "out" years, future fiscal years for which the budget does not apply. Predictably, these future budget cuts rarely materialize. Two-year budgets would force Congress to abide by its budget promises, for at least the following year.

Two-year budgets also could foster less costly multi-year contracts for major defense procurement items. The Congressional Budget Office concludes that multi-year contracts have saved the Department of Defense billions of dollars by enabling the agency to purchase larger quantities of weapons and spare parts at less cost.

— Defining the Federal Role —

Plank 4. Abolish subsidies to businesses from such agencies as Urban Development Action Grants, the Export-Import Bank, and the Small Business Administration.

The federal government provides special subsidies and credit to a few privileged businesses at the expense of most others and out of the pockets of the American taxpayers. Example: Urban Development Action Grants have gone to build luxury hotels for private developers. Example: the Export-Import Bank provides special credit to support the overseas markets of several large American firms, literally paying foreigners to buy their goods. Example: the Small Business Administration provides loan guarantees that benefit only two tenths of one percent of American small businesses in sectors where such aid is not needed.

There is no economic justification for singling out a few businesses for special government handouts. Such pork barrel payments contribute to the federal budget deficit and make it more difficult for other businesses to secure credit for their activities.

Plank 5. Contract out federal services.

In 1955 Dwight Eisenhower signed a presidential directive stating: "The federal government will not start or carry on any commercial activity to provide a service or product for its own use if such product or service can be procured from private enterprise." Since then, the federal government by and large has ignored this directive. Only about 5 percent of the 600,000 government positions identified by the Grace Commission as commercial in nature are contracted out. These include routine activities as data processing, janitorial services, and maintenance.

A greater federal commitment to contracting out would save about $5 billion without reducing the quality of federal services. In the limited federal experience with contracting out, service costs have been slashed by between 20 percent and 50 percent on average. The Department of Defense saved over $600 million in 1986 through competitive contracting. This is a painless approach to deficit reduction, involving no cuts in program activities.

The federal government should follow the lead of the states and cities which rely heavily on the private sector to perform commercial activities for the government. The states and cities with the most successful contracting out programs have reduced the original opposition of public employees significantly by assuring them that they will receive jobs elsewhere in the government, or with the private contractor, if their position is contracted out.

Plank 6. Merge federal aid programs to the states into a single Fiscal Capacity Grant and combine it with a tax cut.

States currently receive federal aid for a multitude of programs, from Medicaid to Urban Development Action Grants. Most of these federal aid programs are based on the alleged needs of individuals or communities, and take little or no account of the economic and fiscal condition of the state itself.

17

To the extent that the federal government should be assisting state and local programs, aid should be channeled only to those states that cannot support necessary programs themselves. The federal government first should specify the programs it is prepared to underwrite and calculate the level of spending needed in each state to achieve the goals of each program. Second, Washington should calculate the "tax capacity" of each state. This is the amount of tax that a state could raise if it were to apply a hypothetical standard state tax code. Third, the federal government should consolidate all its existing aid to state and local government into a Fiscal Capacity Grant and allocate the money according to the difference between a state's tax capacity and the funds it needs for the necessary programs.

Federal support thus would go only to states that lacked the means to finance basic programs. Unlike under the existing structure, it would not go to rich states.

The reform would be welcomed by poor states, but would no doubt run into angry opposition from richer states. To deal with this, the considerable potential savings from the reform should finance an across-the-board tax cut. This would have its greatest impact, and thus greatest popularity, in the states losing most federal aid.

Plank 7. Encourage cities and states to seek private sector financing for infrastructure improvements.

The nation's highways, bridges, airports, waste water treatment plants, and transit systems are in great need of repair. A 1983 study by the Associated General Contractors of America (AGC) predicts that over the next 20 years the states and cities must spend nearly $120 billion to improve their decaying infrastructure. The AGC further estimates that the cities and states will be able to raise only about $50 billion of the necessary capital investment.

Even with federal support, the cities and states will need to turn to the private sector to upgrade the condition of their basic infrastructure. Already pioneering cities and states have begun to contract with private companies to build and operate transit systems and waste water treatment plants. These jurisdictions are discovering that expenditures are on average 30 percent below the cost of government management and control.

Despite these successes, federal regulations typically prohibit private sector ownership and operation of infrastructure. Local jurisdictions often forfeit federal funds when they opt to go private. Such federal regulations are inimical to public works improvement and should be lifted.

19

Plank 8. Privatize federal assets and programs.

The federal government owns or operates many assets and commercial enterprises, ranging from public housing and public lands, to the Postal Service, to the Amtrak passenger railway system. As with nationalized assets in every other country, these American assets are bureaucratized, politicized and poorly maintained; where they have customers, be they public housing tenants, mail users, or train passengers, the customers' interests are always placed below those of the government workers delivering the "service."

The solution to this mess is privatization via employee ownership (for Amtrak and the Postal Service), management or ownership by customers (for public housing) or outright sale (for the loan portfolio).

This privatization would give Americans better services, by exchanging bureaucratic management sensitive to political pressure for private management sensitive to competition and consumers' interests. The change would also save taxpayers' dollars. In cases where inefficient federal management undermines the productivity of workers, privatization would cut losses while improving worker productivity.

Plank 9. Limit federal non-defense spending to 15 percent of GNP by 1992.

The cause of triple digit budget deficits has not been Ronald Reagan's determination to rebuild the U.S. arsenal. Nor has it been the Reagan 1981 tax cuts. Rather, the deficits are the result of the steep and steady rise in the non-defense portion of the federal budget over the past quarter century. Between 1960 and 1986, the percentage of GNP devoted to national defense has dropped from 9.7 percent to 6.5 percent. But over this same period, non-defense spending has doubled from 8.8 percent to 17.7 percent of GNP. From 1980 through 1987, federal revenues grew by 62 percent in real terms. During these same Reagan years, domestic spending increased by $292 billion, outpacing defense increases by $56 billion.

Federal domestic spending must be brought down closer to its historical levels if the federal government hopes to balance the budget in this century. Before 1970 the share of GNP devoted to non-defense spending never exceeded 15 percent. To reach a permanent target of 15 percent by 1992, the next administration should pledge to reduce domestic spending by about one-half of one percent of GNP per year.

—— The Deficit ——

Plank 10. Adopt Grace Commission Reforms.

In 1984, the President's Private Sector Survey on Cost Control, headed by J. Peter Grace, Chairman and Chief Executive Officer of W.R. Grace and Company, identified over 2,000 ways to "eliminate waste, inefficiency, and mismanagement in the federal government." This Grace Commission estimated that its proposals would result in savings of approximately $140 billion per year. Grace Commission recommendations already have saved $39 billion per year, yet over 600 reforms with potential annual savings of almost $70 billion are yet to be adopted.

A General Accounting Office review of the Grace Commission report concluded that "in GAO's opinion about two-thirds of the recommendations have merit." For instance, the report found that of the 3,000 military bases in the U.S., only about 300 are essential for national defense. Closing unnecessary bases could save over $2 billion annually. The Commmission also found that the federal government spends over six times as much on the pension of a civil service employee as the best private companies spend on their workers. Reforms in federal pensions could lower the deficit by over $10 billion.

The Grace Commission report demonstrates clearly that the federal budget remains crammed with wasteful spending. It also demonstrates that the deficit can be conquered in the 1990s without tax hikes, steep cuts in spending for national defense, or by cutting into the government safety net for the poor. The Commission report must be reexamined; its recommendations should be given a high profile by public officials. This might be accomplished by forming a presidential task force to follow up the Grace Commission and to determine the status of its recommendations. As with the original report, this should be financed entirely by the private sector.

Plank 11. Reform the military retirement system.

As compensation for their special service to their country, U.S. military personnel deserve generous retirement benefits. Yet the current military retirement structure is in dire need of reform. Today the program costs four times what it did in 1970. The system's unfunded liability is currently estimated at $500 billion and is growing annually.

The current military retirement system is out of step with the Pentagon's goals of recruiting and retaining essential personnel. Initial recruitment of enlisted soldiers, most of whom are between the ages of 18 and 25, is not greatly enhanced by offering them very lucrative pension benefits. Recruitment efforts might be improved if future retirement benefits were cut, but short-term inducements in the form of higher basic pay were offered.

The retirement system also provides perverse career incentives for highly trained specialists, such as computer technicians and engineers, essential to efficient military operations. The system encourages these specialists to leave the military after 20 years of service, collect their military pension, and transfer their skills to the private sector. They can then become eligible to receive two pensions. Today half of all military retirees leave the service within a year of the 20-year plateau. The retirement system's costs would be lowered, and the efficiency of military operations enhanced, if personnel were given a stronger incentive to stay for 30 rather than 20 years.

Plank 12. Block tax increases for deficit reduction.

The federal deficit is not caused by tax cuts. Taxes as a percentage of GNP under Ronald Reagan are barely below the level under Jimmy Carter. Social Security and other tax hikes already passed by Congress will soon push the tax share of GNP to historic new highs. The culprit is spending, which has continued its remorseless rise.

Those members of Congress who refuse to trim spending seem to think that they can reduce the federal deficit by raising taxes. This almost guarantees higher, not lower, long-term deficits. The expectation of even a temporary deficit reduction would lift what little pressure there is for spending cuts from the shoulders of Congress, leading to a surge of new spending. This is precisely what happened when Congress "cut" the deficit with a tax hike in 1982-- the deficit doubled. What is worse, tax hikes strangle the golden goose. By increasing business costs and throwing Americans out of work, they reduce tax revenues while increasing the demand for government services. This adds to deficit pressures. Tax increases are no solution to deficits. Only spending reductions reduce deficits.

Plank 13. Establish a commission to review all entitlements programs.

Spending on entitlements has grown rapidly in recent decades. Between 1960 and 1981, federal means-tested benefit programs increased by more than 640 percent in real terms, from $16 billion in 1960 to $102 billion in 1985 (in 1985 constant dollars). During the Reagan Administration, spending on federal means-tested benefit programs grew, in real terms, from $74 billion in 1980 to $97 billion in 1985. Since the mid-1950s, outlays on Social Security, unemployment insurance, federal pensions, and similar programs increased fivefold, in real terms, from $90 billion to $445 billion over the same period. Ronald Reagan has failed to cut entitlements; he merely has slowed growth in such needs-based entitlements as Medicaid and public housing.

What is needed is a fundamental reassessment of federal obligations and a corresponding restructuring of federal programs. Since Congress is unwilling, or politically unable, to tackle this explosive issue, a blue ribbon, bipartisan Commission on Entitlements may be able to do so.

The commission should consider: the purpose of entitlements; how specific entitlement policy goals can be reached most efficiently; to what is society entitled in exchange for individual entitlements; the social benefit of particular entitlements; how responsibilities for entitlements should be divided among the various levels of government; to what degree do entitlement programs foster American values, such as individual freedom, social responsibility, the work ethic, and personal independence; and whether various entitlement programs with the same goal should be consolidated.

* * *

STRATEGY

Federal spending is out of control. Enormous deficits undermine U.S. economic strength and mortgage the country's future. Many federal spending policies benefit Washington politicians and bureaucrats more than the American public. Conservatives seek fairness, efficiency, and restraint in federal spending to give security and opportunity to all Americans. Conservatives also recognize that sometimes the private sector is a better vehicle to pursue a public policy goal than is the public sector. And even when government is the answer, it is far better to utilize the level of government closest to the people concerned than to turn to Washington.

The federal deficit is not caused by tax cuts. By speeding growth, tax rate reductions led to a boost in revenues, especially from higher income earners. The real culprit has been spending. Despite talk of bringing the deficit under control, and despite actual cuts in defense, Congress refuses to take determined action to bring domestic spending under control.

27

OBSTACLES

The dynamics of the U.S. political system measures a politician's value by the gross number of federal dollars he or she delivers to constituents. This makes it politically dangerous for politicians to say "no" to spending. Three essential components fuel this dynamic. First is the fairness issue, the mindset that certain groups and individuals are "entitled" to federal expenditures. The liberal welfare state has transformed the notion that government has a responsibility to provide for the common good of its people to a creed that the federal government must redistribute wealth to meet social goals. Those who receive federal benefits resist spending reforms which they perceive will end their entitlement.

The second component is the spending coalition that blocks significant reform. Powerful lobbyists and special interest groups draw on the fears of beneficiaries and raise the compassion issue to mobilize opposition to reform. Third, are the politicians. Their ability to dip into the federal Treasury to placate constituents and reward allies yields the votes and political power that keep them in office.

TACTICS

Redefine the Spending Debate. *Liberals must not be allowed to define conservative solutions as retreats from com-*

passion or fairness. On the contrary, conservative spending proposals offer compassionate solutions to the failures of the welfare state. They offer fairness to the American taxpayer by eliminating wasteful budget processes and inefficient bureaucracies. They offer opportunity by introducing new flexibility to spending and innovative alternatives to federal handouts. The primary focus of the 1988 spending debate should be on constructing federal policies that do a better job of fulfilling government's obligation to assist the needy and provide meaningful opportunity to all Americans.

Publicize Waste and Inefficiency. *Politicians must be made accountable for the waste and special interest payoffs embedded in congressional spending. The public must be informed of the failures of the congressional spending process, typified by the pork-packed Continuing Resolution enacted just before Congress's 1987 Christmas recess. Efforts to educate the public should coincide with periods of major congressional action on spending. When Congress begins considering the budget, for example, conservatives should hold press conferences at key junctures in the process. Consideration of the debt limit in 1988 should trigger efforts to increase public awareness of the need for reform.*

Take a Stand on the Debt Ceiling. *Gramm-Rudman-Hollings, the only major budget reform in the past decade, was passed as an amendment to a debt ceiling bill. The 1988 debt ceiling bill should be used to force Congress to reform* *its spending process. Fundamental budget reform must be the price Congress pays for raising the federal debt ceiling once again.*

Mobilize Grass Roots Efforts for Specific Reforms. *To move Washington toward budget reform, specific policy goals such as the balanced budget amendment and line-item veto should be pursued at the grass roots level. Public resentment and anger toward current policies can be channeled to Congress through agitation for these specific reforms. This effort should parallel the 1970s' anti-tax movement.*

Require a Tax Pledge. *During the 1986 elections, candidates and office holders were given the opportunity either to sign or disavow a pledge not to increase taxes. The pledge was signed by a number of Democrat and GOP candidates. This tax pledge effort should be revived and expanded in 1988. Public awareness of the pledge needs to be heightened so that politicians are held accountable for their views toward taxes.*

Break the Link Between Taxes and Deficit Cuts. *The alleged link between deficit reduction and tax increases must be severed. A litany of past tax increases and their application to deficit reduction should be documented. Example: The 1982 Tax Equity and Fiscal Responsibility Act (TEFRA) agreement pledged three dollars in spending cuts*

30

for every one dollar raised in taxes. Congress, however, raised the taxes but did not reduce spending.

Offer Alternatives. *Too often in the past, conservatives proposed spending cuts without offering alternatives to better serve the intended purposes of federal spending. In 1988, spending solutions should emphasize more efficient alternatives to massive federal spending, such as privatization and greater control at state and local levels.*

Explain How Privatization Benefits Workers. *Privatization offers workers tangible ownership interests in enterprises formally owned by the government. Plank 8, for example, proposes privatization of the Postal Service. Book value of the Postal Service is estimated at $7 billion. Privatization could give each postal employee an opportunity to purchase a part of those assets at a substantial discount. Conservatives should form a National Committee for Postal Worker Opportunity to push for privatization reforms that will benefit workers. The Committee could issue sample stock certificates that would guarantee each worker a certain portion of Postal Service assets upon passage of privatization legislation in Congress.*

31

COALITION FOR VICTORY

Taxpayers. *The American taxpayer is the biggest loser in Washington's current spending policies. Federal revenues have increased by 50 percent since 1981 and yet taxpayers are faced with a $148 billion deficit. Taxpayers want their dollars spent efficiently on security, services, and assistance to those in need. Reforming the congressional budget process and encouraging more efficient alternatives to bureaucratic spending programs will restore value to tax-payer expenditures. From California's Proposition 13 to the current quest for a constitutional convention on a balanced budget, experience has shown that American taxpayers can be mobilized when they see that politicians are taking unfair advantage of them, and when they are presented with a specific plan of action. The no-tax pledge will force politicians to take sides "for" or "against" the taxpayer.*

State and local governments. *While cutbacks in federal assistance would be unpopular in most states, many key states would support a streamlining and an overhaul of the grants system through the Fiscal Equity Grant proposal. First, it would appeal to less affluent states, because federal assistance would be concentrated in those states that need help, rather than spread thinly throughout the country. And second, while richer states would lose federal aid, their tax-payers would benefit from the tax reduction tied to the grant* *proposal. Thus potential opposition from richer states would be muted.*

Businesses and Workers. *The privatization of government assets means real opportunities for specific firms and workers. The proposal in 1986 and 1987 to sell Conrail and part of the federal loan portfolio, for example, aroused strong interest from sectors seeing such privatization as a business opportunity. This ultimately helped to assure passage of those proposals. The planks to privatize further assets and to contract out government services similarly should spark the commercial interest of many workers, businesses, and business organizations.*

Chapter Two

Taxes and Business

The economic high growth 1980s demonstrate that the way to create jobs and prosperity is not by government manipulation of the economy through controls or special benefits to selected industries, but by creating an environment that stimulates enterprise. Giving a green light to growth means tax incentives for savings and risk-taking, removal of barriers to competition, and low inflation.

To keep the light green, the U.S. needs to continue the work begun during the Reagan Administration. First, the tax code must eliminate taxes on savings and foster investment. This could be achieved by moving closer to an "expenditure" tax. Second, deregulation of the economy must continue to boost competition in a way that benefits innovative businessmen and consumers. In particular, artificial restrictions on banking, the lifeblood of free enterprise, must be removed. Third, the federal government should privatize its loan portfolio to reduce its distortions of the credit markets.

Plank 14. Create a Commission on Economic Growth to emphasize growth-oriented policies.

The rationale behind sound economic and fiscal policy is to foster economic growth by restraining the growth of government. But the appeal of this policy to most Americans is undermined because they tend not to appreciate the importance of long-term economic growth in improving their current and future standard of living. Instead, they are often sidetracked into accepting short-term policies, such as tax increases to "solve" the deficit, which hurt growth. Yet economic growth has raised the standard of living of the average American this century by 800 percent after adjustment for inflation.

A Commission should be established to raise public consciousness concerning the importance of economic growth and to establish growth as the number one goal of economic policy. The Commission, drawn from business organizations and pro-growth citizens groups, also should explore policies for increasing the U.S. growth rate.

The Commission on Economic Growth should underscore the fact that with a real per capita growth rate of 5 percent per annum, an average family's income will double in fourteen years, while at a one percent growth rate it would take 70 years for the same increase to occur. The Commission should stress that nations with lower rates of government spending have higher rates of economic growth. Example: an extra $1.00 in government spending today will reduce the GNP by $5.00 just ten years in the future. The work of the Commission on Economic Growth should be reinforced by creating permanent high-level offices on economic growth in the White House, the Office of Management and Budget, and the Treasury Department.

—— Income Taxes ——

Plank 15. Reduce the capital gains tax rate from 28 percent to 15 percent.

In an effort to "raise" revenue, the Tax Reform Act of 1986 increased the top tax rate on capital gains from 20 percent to 28 percent. This ignores historical experience, which teaches that higher capital gains taxes yield lower revenues. Higher capital gains taxes also inhibit the efficient use of capital and discourage entrepreneurial ventures and the development of new technologies.

According to a study by Harvard economist Lawrence Lindsay, reducing the capital gains tax to 15 percent could raise additional revenues of $8 billion in fiscal year 1988, $11 billion in 1989, and $12 billion in 1990. The Steiger Amendment of 1978, which nearly halved the capital gains tax, boosted capital gains revenue by 44 percent between 1977 and 1979.

It also may be wise to eliminate capital gains taxes altogether. Such taxes diminish an incentive for the long-term investments that are crucial for economic growth. Foreign competitors have already taken such a step. West Germany, Japan, Hong Kong, the Republic of China on Taiwan, and South Korea exempt long-term investments from capital gains taxation.

Plank 16. Reduce taxes which discourage savings by expanding IRAs and insuring Family Investment Plans.

Savings rates in the U.S. are the lowest among the major industrial nations in large part because the tax code taxes savings twice: first when it is accumulated through earnings and again when such saving earns interest. The result: it is twice as costly to save as it is to consume.

One of the best vehicles for increasing private saving is the Individual Retirement Account (IRA). Economists David Wise of Harvard and Steven Venti of Dartmouth find that 45 percent to 55 percent of IRA contributions constituted new savings. This allows individuals to obtain a tax deduction for deposits made into such accounts and allows interest and profits earned on such deposits during the working life of the taxpayer to accumulate tax free. In the Tax Reform Act of 1986, however, most workers lost the deductions for IRA contributions.

The IRA deduction should be restored and expanded. The maximum annual fully tax deductible IRA contribution limit should be increased from $2,000 to $2,500 for all workers. Spouses not employed outside the home should be allowed to make the same $2,500 contribution per year as their employed partners. Homemakers, after all, have the same retirement needs as others. Restoring the full use of IRAs would provide tax incentives to stimulate saving, thereby providing the capital necessary to finance U.S. economic expansion.

In addition, the U.S. should establish Family Investment Plans, following the examples of Britain and Japan, which have made it more attractive for small investors to save.

In Japan, small savers may earn interest tax free in so-called postal accounts. In Britain, "personal equity plans" permit individuals to invest a limited amount in stocks and bonds entirely free of tax on interest, dividends, and capital gains. Both Japan and Britain enjoy substantially higher savings rates than the U.S.

Plank 17. Increase personal exemptions and fund this by repealing the federal deduction for state and local taxes.

Despite the increase in the personal exemption to $2,000 under the 1986 tax reform legislation, the federal tax burden still falls more heavily on families than it did at the end of World War II. If the personal exemption of $600 in the 1940s had been indexed for inflation and taxes, it would be over $5,000 today. The dramatic increase since the 1940s in Social Security payroll taxes that are not subject to personal exemptions has raised the total federal tax burden on families even more. These tax trends have also fallen particularly harshly on lower income workers. To remedy this, personal exemptions should be increased by at least $1,000.

The revenue that this will lose for the federal Treasury could be offset in great part by removing deductions for state and local taxes. These deductions have encouraged higher state and local taxes.

—— Deregulation ——

Plank 18. Remove barriers to interstate banking.

The 1927 McFadden Act and the 1956 Douglas Amendment to the Bank Holding Company Act constitute the framework for the regulation of interstate banking. Under these laws, banks face severe restrictions on their ability to diversify geographically. The problem with this is that a bank's soundness and safety are seriously jeopardized when its loan portfolio becomes too concentrated in one sector of the economy — such as energy or agriculture. The recent wave of bank failures in the farm belt and oil patch states painfully confirm this. Relaxing the restrictions on interstate banking would enable a bank to diversify its loan portfolio, reducing the share of loans concentrated within a particular industry or geographic area.

The current bank regulatory framework rests on the premise that restricting interstate banking increases competition in local markets by ensuring that large interstate banks could not overwhelm smaller banks. Experience teaches, in fact, that interstate mergers tend to improve competition in local markets. Mergers often enable local banks to operate more efficiently through better management procedures and economies of scale. In addition, new products and services are introduced into the local market.

Restrictions on interstate banking weaken the U.S. banking system and reduce the efficiency of the economy generally. Greater competition and regional diversification would strengthen the system and lead to fewer bank failures. The McFadden Act and the Douglas Amendment therefore should be repealed.

Plank 19. Repeal the Glass-Steagall Act, which separates commercial and investment banking.

The Glass-Steagall Act of 1933 separates banking institutions into investment banks, which underwrite stock offerings and deal in securities, and commercial banks, which primarily take deposits and lend money. This law reduces American banking's international competitiveness and undermines the ability of the economy to finance business.

42

Ranked by assets, only one U.S. commercial bank, Citicorp, is among the world's top ten. U.S. commercial banks are even prevented under current law from competing against certain European and Japanese banks within America's borders, since a number of foreign banks are exempt from Glass-Steagall banking restrictions. Foreign banks now provide over 20 percent of all loans made to U.S. businesses and are increasingly active in domestic corporate debt and equity underwriting.

To allow American banks to compete in the world financial markets, to lower transaction costs, and promote the freer flow of funds, Glass-Steagall should be repealed.

Plank 20. Resist regulations hindering corporate takeovers.

Competition for control of corporations enhances the competitiveness of U.S. business. Corporate takeovers are beneficial. For one thing, they break up inefficient conglomerates. For another, they prod managers to invest in long-range projects that make economic sense, revitalize faltering companies, reallocating assets to more·productive uses and increasing shareholder wealth. These benefits deliver products and services to the consumer at a lower cost, thus benefiting the economy in general and individuals and families in particular. In 1984 and 1985 alone, stockholders earned nearly $75 billion in premiums as a result of takeovers.

Some takeovers, to be sure, have involved abuse. Corporate "raiders" as well as managements have been guilty in these instances. There are ways, however, to protect stockholders from such practices, such as stockholders amending the corporate charter and various court remedies. What is not needed is sweeping new legislation to hamstring the takeover process. The market is a more accurate judge than the government of whether or not a takeover is in the best interests of stockholders.

—— Government Loans ——

Plank 21. Sell federal direct loan originations to private buyers.

The federal government originates between $40 billion and $50 billion in direct loans each year. As America's largest financial intermediary, federal agencies now carry over $250 billion worth of outstanding direct loans. The government guarantees an additional $450 billion in private loans. Federal loans contain various types of implicit subsidies to the borrower, including below-market interest rates and terms, as well as generous provisions regarding foreclosure.

Defaults on federal loans occur four times as often as they do for loans made by private lenders. Collection rates are dismal. Interest rate subsidies and contingent liabilities are either improperly accounted for or (as in the case of guarantees) totally unaccounted for. Moreover, there are no uniform procedures for calculating what these loans are actually worth to the federal government. These structural problems are unlikely to be rectified by management changes. The answer to the problems plaguing federal lending practices is to transfer ownership of the portfolio to the private sector where routine business procedures can be applied and politicized accounting eliminated.

Selling new loans would reform federal credit management in several ways. First, selling new loans would provide a market value for the loans. The difference between the face value of the loan and its sale price would reflect the subsidy inherent in the loan. Second, debt collection would improve as the private owner would have a greater incentive to track down delinquent debtors. Third, loan documentation would improve in order to enhance the sale price of the loans. Fourth, the federal government would save money as it would no longer have to service the loans.

The sale of the loans must be on a non-recourse basis, which means the loans must be sold without a federal guarantee. The absence of federal guarantees will insure that creditors adequately police the loans to collect payment and prevent default. During fiscal 1987, the federal government raised $3.8 billion through a loan sale pilot program. The sales demonstrate that such a program will work.

Plank 22. Reinsure government loan guarantees with private insurance.

A federal loan guarantee is a pledge by the government to pay to the banks that make the loans the principal and in some cases the interest in event of borrower default. Federal loan guarantees have grown enormously. In 1975, the U.S. guaranteed about $30 billion in loans; in 1987, it was $160 billion worth. The government now has $450 billion in outstanding guarantees.

Loan guarantees are contingent liabilities. Because the federal government utilizes a cash budget, contingent liabilities do not show up in the budget. This provides a perverse incentive for Congress to encourage federal guarantees as a "free" means of providing federal credit. Yet guarantees are far from free. In 1986, for instance, the federal government appropriated over $8 billion to pay off lenders who held defaulted federally guaranteed loans.

To reduce its default exposure as well as to determine the subsidy implicit in a guaranteed loan, the federal government should purchase reinsurance for all loans it guarantees. By privately reinsuring guarantees, the cost of the private guarantee would make its impact on the budget the year that the subsidy was provided. The subsidy would equal the cost of the reinsurance.

*　　*　　*

STRATEGY

Americans are empowered and liberty is promoted by allowing individuals the greatest freedom to use their own assets and the fruits of their labor. Taxes and regulation stifle competition and economic growth by limiting business and consumer choices. Meanwhile, government taxation of individuals empowers government with increased revenues *while limiting individual and family choices by discouraging savings and reducing take-home pay. Conservative solutions, therefore, center on reducing government regulation and taxation. The economic growth of the 1980s demonstrates how reductions in individual taxes and government regulation of the economy can fuel business expansion and individual achievement.*

OBSTACLES

Relief from excessive taxation and regulation faces twin obstacles. First, a Congress which finished major tax reform in 1986 will be reluctant to move forward with additional changes in 1988. Second, institutional forces inside and outside government that benefit from current tax and regulatory policies will resist change. The politicians and interest groups who believe in big government solutions, for example, will oppose elimination of the state sales tax deduction, because this will force states to become leaner. Politicians who believe in the power of government rather than the power of the free market will oppose reductions in capital gains tax.

TACTICS

As the 1986 tax revision takes full effect in 1988, public awareness of tax reform will be heightened. A strong public sentiment for further action could emerge.

Emphasize Economic Benefits of Tax Cuts. *The relationship between the economic growth of the 1980s and the tax reduction policies of the Reagan era must be thoroughly documented. The public needs to be educated on how tax cuts have benefited them directly in the past seven years. Tax cuts, for instance, have increased consumer purchasing power. Consumer groups should be encouraged to support further tax changes that will further benefit them. Workers, meanwhile, must be taught the connection between their employment and tax policies in Washington. Tax incentives for businesses mean more jobs and better wages for workers. Reductions in personal income taxes mean more take-home pay for workers. Thus, organized labor should make tax reduction a primary goal for 1988.*

Show How Tax Cuts Reduce the Deficit. *"Tax cut" should replace "tax hike" in the litany of deficit reduction. The notion should be dispelled that tax cuts have contributed to the federal deficit. Since the Reagan tax cuts of 1981, for example, federal revenues have increased by 50 percent; the problem is that spending has grown by 54 percent.*

Build Support for Deregulating the Financial Industry. *Reduced regulation in the financial industry gives the consumer more choice and tougher competition, which forces down the price of services. Consumers must be shown the inefficiencies in the current system and the benefits of deregulation. America's farm and energy sectors, for ex-*

ample, have been buffeted by the inability of local banks to weather economic downturns. Relaxing the restrictions on interstate banking will foster more diversified and hence stronger banks in these local communities. Bank customers in rural America also will recognize the enhanced level of service which can be provided through the increased competition of interstate banking.

The public also must be made aware of the relationship between growing foreign influence in financial markets and anti-competitive restrictions on banks. Failure to remove restriction on American banks means financial decisions affecting the U.S. economy increasingly will be made in Tokyo rather than New York or San Francisco. The result will be a loss of jobs in the U.S. financial industry and more foreign ownership of U.S. businesses.

Dispel negative notions of corporate takeovers. *The consumer and shareholder benefits of takeovers must be emphasized. Particular takeovers in recent years must be analyzed thoroughly in terms of direct economic benefits such as consumer prices and choices, jobs, and shareholder profit. These case studies will provide the basis for mobilizing business, consumer and labor coalitions behind a responsible view of corporate takeovers.*

50

COALITION FOR VICTORY

The Poor. *An increase in the personal exemption tax would be of substantial benefit to low income workers, freeing thousands of poorer families from paying federal income taxes. Conservatives, who believe in empowering the poor, will be joined by truly compassionate liberals in support of this effort.*

The Elderly. *Because they live off savings, the elderly are hardest hit by taxation of those savings. Taxing savings, in effect, is the same as cutting Social Security benefits. Both actions take away from the elderly money that has been saved over their lifetime and to which they are entitled. Organizations which represent retired persons should push for repeal of this confiscatory policy with the same zeal they exhibit on Social Security issues. That most elderly persons live on fixed incomes also means that an increase in the personal exemption would have a substantially greater impact on them than on other taxpayers. Those organizations and individuals who truly represent the interests of the elderly should back Plank 16 vigorously.*

The Family. *Increasing the personal exemptions will mean greater tax relief for families with children. Family savings for education, and other major expenditures, meanwhile, will be enhanced by eliminating the double taxation of* savings. *And husbands and wives planning for retirement will be encouraged to make retirement arrangements by restoring full IRA deductions, indexing the deductible limit, and allowing spouses working in the home a full IRA deduction. Conservatives and liberals who believe in restoring the strength of the family should support these proposals.*

Baby Boom Workers. *Younger workers, particularly those now planning for their retirement have a substantial interest in more favorable tax treatment of IRAs. Many of these younger workers rightly question whether Social Security will be there for them when they retire.*

The Financial Industry. *Banks and other financial institutions will benefit from tax incentives for savings. Increasing the personal deduction and reducing capital gains taxes will transfer dollars from the public to the private sector, stimulating the investment that sustains the financial industry. The financial industry can play a major role in mobilizing the tax cut coalition. Elements of the coalition were energized during the successful 1982 effort to repeal the withholding of taxes from savings. In addition, the financial industry is a powerful ally in winning reform of banking laws and in privatizing the loan portfolio. Deregulation of financial institutions means the prospect of huge new markets for firms kept out of certain activities by federal law. Financial institutions, moreover, played a central role in winning approval in Congress for the sale of some federal loan assets.*

Chapter Three

Labor

A freely functioning labor market, with unions accurately representing workers who choose to join them, and wage rates reflecting employer-employee bargaining, is good for American workers and the best recipe for a competitive economy. Current laws, however, force reluctant workers to join unions and tend to impose high union pay scales on many firms inducing non-competitiveness and job loss. In addition, legislative proposals to introduce "comparable worth" schemes and to force employers to provide numerous benefits would undermine the basic foundations of America's market economy and threaten the jobs of many Americans.

A constructive U.S. labor policy should: 1) end costly union rates on federal projects; 2) enshrine in law the worker's right not to belong to a union; 3) encourage states to pass Right-To-Work laws; 4) resist efforts to introduce comparable worth dogmas into pay scales to shift the costs of life style choices onto American business.

—— Workers' Rights ——

Plank 23. Reaffirm the right of the employee to join or not join labor unions.

Section 7 of the National Labor Relations Act (NLRA), entitled "Rights of Employees," states:

> Employees shall have the right to self-organization to form, join or assist labor organizations, to bargain collectively through representatives of their own choosing, and to engage in other concerted activities for the purpose of collective bargaining or other mutual aid or protection, *and shall also have the right to refrain from any or all such activities...* (emphasis added).

For more than four decades the overwhelming majority of Americans have defended the right of employees to get and hold their jobs regardless of whether they join or support a union. Forcing a worker to join or pay dues equivalents to an unwanted union amounts to deprivation of the First Amendment guarantee of freedom of association, the Fifth and Fourteenth Amendments' guarantee of due process over matters affecting life, liberty and property and the Thirteenth Amendment guarantee of freedom from involuntary servitude.

Even Section 7 of the NLRA, as cited above, reaffirms these basic rights. Yet, Section 7 goes on to limit the right to refrain from any or all union activities, by granting the right:

> ..except to the extent that such right may be affected by an agreement requiring union membership as a condition of employment....

This double-talk in Section 7 makes a mockery of employee rights. Accordingly, an employee has full freedom of rights except when compulsory unionism enters the picture. This exception clause should be repealed.

Plank 24. Ban diversion of union dues to political or ideological purposes if employees object.

The U.S. Supreme Court recently ruled that unions, as exclusive bargaining agents, cannot use proceeds from dues to pursue political or ideological goals over the objections of affected employees. The proceeds from those employees, says the Court, are to be used strictly for collective bargaining and contract administration, including grievance adjustment. (See *Machinists v. Street*, 1961 and *Ellis v. Railway Clerks*, 1984.)

Dues are mandatory even for employees who are not members of the union but who may be required, under the National Labor Relations Act principle of exclusive representation, to support the union. Federal legislation is needed to require the written authorization of workers for unions to use dues or dues equivalents for political purposes. A "Workers Political Involvement Act" should be enacted to place the burden on unions to prove that no funds are being diverted without written consent.

Plank 25. Empower federal authorities to prosecute violence or the threat of violence in labor disputes.

In 1946 Congress enacted the Hobbs Anti-Extortion Act to end what was then widespread violence during industrial labor disputes. In 1973, however, the U.S. Supreme Court, in its 5-4 *Enmons* decision, ruled that violence on an industrial site by a union does not constitute a federal crime if it is employed in furtherance of a "legitimate" union objective. The result has been a renewed surge of union violence, especially in the construction, transportation, and coal industries. State prohibitions of such violence and extortion have proved to be dubious deterrents. One reason for this is the unresolved question of whether such state prohibitions apply to companies that are located in the state but engage in interstate commerce. Individual states cannot handle union violence when it crosses state lines.

Federal legislation is needed to reverse the *Enmons* decision and make union threats, extortion, intimidation, mass picketing, physical force, and other forms of violence a federal crime, with the states having concurrent jurisdiction.

—— **Labor Reform** ——

Plank 26. Restore flexibility to public sector pay.

In 1983, the U.S. General Accounting Office, an arm of Congress, issued a report entitled "The Davis-Bacon Act Should be Repealed." The report concluded that Davis-Bacon requirements add $2 billion annually to federal construction contracts. The 1931 Davis-Bacon Act requires that workers on public projects be paid "prevailing" wages.

Originally the Davis-Bacon Act applied only to direct federal construction projects, but subsequent amendments extended the coverage to include federally assisted construction projects involving housing, health, transportation, pollution control, and revenue sharing.

Current Davis-Bacon enforcement in effect discriminates against small nonunion contractors bidding on government jobs. One reason is the difficulty of paying a worker union scale one week and a different wage the next week when working on a private contract. Another reason is that small businesses often cannot afford the clerical, legal, and accounting staffs to cope with the paperwork required by the government. The Davis-Bacon Act should be repealed.

Plank 27. Reject gender-based pay scales.

"Comparable worth" is a fashionable new concept based on the unproven premise that the marketplace pays unfairly low wages to workers in traditional female occupations such as secretaries or nurses. To remedy this putative wrong, comparable worth backers want government bureaucracies and the courts to set wages. There is no evidence, however, that the market systematically underpays workers in traditional female jobs.

Comparable worth seeks to replace wage rates based on the objective factors of supply and demand with a wage setting process which is purely subjective. Under such a system, fair wages would be determined by the personal biases of so-called job evaluators. Because comparable wage controls are often set arbitrarily, the results are often bizarre. Example: a system in Wisconsin determined that typists should be given higher ratings than aircraft pilots on the basis that the "consequences of error" in the former profession are greater than in the latter.

The economic consequences of comparable worth would be devastating. A recent study by the National

Bureau of Economic Research predicts that an economy-wide comparable worth policy could result in a loss of between 2.8 and 4 million jobs and a reduction in the gross national product of up to $150 billion per annum. Comparable worth also is unlikely to benefit female workers. Artificially raising wages in traditional female jobs above market rates will simply cause employers to cut down on the number of such jobs available. The result will be a serious increase in unemployment for the least advantaged female workers. Thus, comparable worth policy may well cause a net loss in female income.

The economic interests of women are best served by ending discrimination which bars women from traditionally male-dominated jobs. Comparable worth does not advance economic opportunities for women and will harm the economy; it should be strongly resisted.

Plank 28. Promote employment opportunities by reforming minimum wage laws.

The federal minimum wage for various economic sectors is currently $3.35 an hour. Legal minimum wages do not alleviate poverty, nor do they improve the conditions of the working poor. By making the least skilled labor more costly, minimum wage laws eliminate jobs for many marginal workers and thus drive them into unemployment. The minimum wage denies jobs to low-skilled Americans, such as inner-city black teenagers.

New employment opportunities will be created by repealing or reforming minimum wage laws. The damaging effects of the minimum wage could be reduced by lowering the number of workers covered by its provisions, by freezing the adult minimum wage at the current level, and by establishing a new "apprentice-level wage" for teenagers. Such changes would increase employment, on-the-job training, and fringe benefit opportunities for American workers.

Plank 29. Expand Americans' right to work at home.

The Home Work Rule of the 1938 Fair Labor Standards Act bans the sale of certain items made or worked on at home. This ban makes little economic sense. For one thing, it forces potential workers to remain idle, limiting America's economic output. For another, it violates the basic right of Americans to work as they please in their own homes. It is particularly harmful to mothers wishing to enter the labor market. Often these women have little or no choice except to work at home because they have preschool children who need supervision. The ban also disproportionately harms workers in rural areas who cannot easily obtain part-time jobs in businesses close to their isolated residences. The handicapped and elderly who cannot get out for regular jobs are also penalized by restrictions on work at home.

Restrictions on the production at home of six categories of products — women's apparel, jewelry, gloves and mittens, buttons and buckles, handkerchiefs, and embroideries — were first issued over 40 years ago. Federal restrictions on work in the home should be rescinded. Home-based workers deserve the freedom enjoyed by Americans in other industries to work where they want and contract their labor as they see fit.

✳   ✳   ✳

STRATEGY

Labor policy should promote jobs, encourage economic growth, induce higher real wages, and safeguard the rights of union and non-union workers alike. Sound labor policies are ratified by the consumer in the marketplace. If consumers do not purchase, business does not profit and workers have no jobs. Similarly, if business does not invest and otherwise boost productivity, wages will stagnate, if not evaporate.

Conservative solutions call for restoring flexibility to labor policies to meet the needs of all workers and encourage innovation in a rapidly changing world economy. Labor policies should be designed to benefit the individual worker, not powerful union leaders. They should not be "pro" or "anti-union," but rather, "pro-worker." And as American industries, entrepreneurs, and workers strive to meet the competitive demands of this new era of global competition, rigid labor laws of a bygone era should not hold them back.

OBSTACLES

An iron triangle of unions, legislators, and bureaucrats stands in the way of innovative labor reform. Labor unions seek to preserve their power on two fronts. First, they work to protect laws such as the compulsory union provisions of the Wagner and Norris-LaGuardia Acts which give them power. Second, they push for new laws which will mandate benefits to employees. Labor unions alone would not be able to thwart labor reform. They are helped by an entrenched bureaucracy at the federal, state, and big-city levels from the U. S. Department of Labor and the National Labor Relations Board down, and by politicians beholden to unions for political support.

TACTICS

Identify the Costs of Rigid Labor Laws. *The American public needs to be informed of the costs of inflexible labor laws. The relationship between labor policies and economic growth must be clearly demonstrated. Rigid labor laws make America poorer. The consumer costs of labor laws and the burdens on small businesses due to bureaucratic over-regulation need to be spelled out. Examples of barriers to work at home should be identified as should other policies which represent payoffs to powerful special interests at the expense of individual productivity and free enterprise. These costs of inefficient labor policies need to be personalized so that the public understands their direct and harmful impact.*

Distinguish Pro-Worker From Pro-Union Policies. *The right of unions to exist is uncontested. Freedom of association is guaranteed by the First Amendment. But it does not follow that workers should be compelled to join a union or pay dues equivalents to it.*

Make Jobs The Issue. *Only profitable companies create jobs; only competitive industries are profitable. A flexible labor policy that encourages growth and spurs competition is the most fundamental right of workers. Labor policies that fail to do this do not serve workers. The shrinking of major traditional manufacturing industries in recent years* *demonstrates how union policies which extract short-term benefits for workers may destroy workers' jobs in the long run.*

Union policies can also destroy workers' incentives and pride. In an industry dominated by restrictive labor policies, a worker's performance has little bearing on his or her job security; job security depends more on political deals struck in Washington. There is little dignity for workers in such jobs.

Publicize Success Stories. *Several sectors of the economy are prospering in an environment free of restrictive labor policies. These success stories need to be publicized. In the steel industry, for example, small, efficient non-union companies such as Florida Steel and Nucor of North Carolina, have seized a growing share of the domestic industry from such giants as Bethlehem and U.S. Steel (USX). Joint ventures by U.S. and Japanese companies, such as between Toyota and GM in Fremont, California, also should be used to highlight the benefits of a new kind of employee-employer relations. States such as North Carolina which encourage cottage industries through flexible labor policies should be singled out for attention.*

COALITION FOR VICTORY

Workers. *U.S. union membership has declined by more than one-half from its post-war high of 35.5 percent of the* *workforce. Since 1979, union membership has declined by 4 million, despite job growth of 13 million. Most American workers thus are not union members. They should back policies which offer the economic flexibility and job security that big labor and big government policies lack.*

Consumers. *Labor policies that encourage competition result in high quality, lower priced goods and services. These policies make consumers the winners.*

Families. *Repealing barriers to work at home strengthens the family. It allows families to maintain dual incomes while avoiding expensive child care costs and giving their children the benefits of maternal care. Other advantages include elimination of the time and expense of commuting to and from work and the use of home personal computers for income-producing work.*

The Disadvantaged. *Labor policies based on productivity and competitiveness will expand job opportunities for all Americans and create new jobs which help the poor. Repealing minimum wage laws will create many new jobs for young workers. This will especially benefit minority youths who have a much higher rate of unemployment than non-minority youths. Handicapped individuals and the elderly, who have difficulty working outside the home, will be empowered by an end to restrictions on work at home.*

Industry. *American businesses will welcome changes in restrictive labor policies which limit their ability to compete. Small businesses will benefit since they are least able to meet costly regulations and still maintain profits. Restoring workers' choice and industry flexibility will enhance competition, creating more growth, new jobs, and better wages.*

Women. *Union leadership remains a male-dominated bastion of patronage. As women seek to have the same opportunities in the marketplace as men, the hierarchy of organized labor remains largely closed to them. Groups concerned about removing barriers to women in the work place should be concerned with removing such barriers within unions themselves.*

Chapter Four

Competitiveness

Rumors of the death of American competitiveness are greatly exaggerated. The U.S. economy is highly productive and efficient. Nevertheless, success in a free enterprise world comes only from eternal vigilance, with countries seeking ways of fostering greater efficiency and innovation within their borders. The U.S., therefore, should be pursuing polices to give American business greater freedom to compete in world markets. To accomplish this, action is needed on three fronts. First, domestic tax and regulatory policies should promote risk taking and innovation, and remove unnecessary business costs. Second, legal impediments to the ability of U.S. firms to compete internationally should be removed. In particular, action should be taken to ease the antitrust laws, to allow U.S. businesses to merge and cooperate where they face tough international competition; to reform liability laws, thereby reducing uncertainty and crippling costs; and to reform international agreements and the Freedom of Information Act to protect the fruits of invention. Third, unemployment and education policies should be revised to assure a well-educated, flexible, and mobile American workforce.

— Tax and Regulatory Reform —

Plank 30. Cut marginal tax rates to stimulate risk-taking and small business ventures.

Marginal tax rates are an important determinant of business activities. High marginal rates mean that for each additional dollar earned by businesses or by individuals, a greater percentage goes to the government. This discourages productive economic activity. The negative effects of high marginal rates especially affect small businesses. The economic risks of such ventures are high. Therefore the promise of profits is crucial to those who risk their money and efforts by setting up new enterprises.

Cutting marginal tax rates on businesses would encourage greater risk-taking and new business ventures. Further, since most small businesses are financed from the savings of the businessmen themselves, the elimination of taxes on interest earned on savings would also encourage greater business formation.

Plank 31. Repeal the Corporate Average Fuel Economy standards on U.S. auto companies.

The 1975 Corporate Average Fuel Economy (CAFE) standards were meant to promote fuel economy. Under these standards, the average gasoline mileage for all cars sold by a given company has to meet an annually rising standard. The CAFE standards threaten the U.S. auto industry. The reason: since 1984, Americans have turned increasingly to larger cars because of lower gas prices and the success of American auto makers in producing fuel-efficient, high quality, less costly cars. Yet, CAFE is not calculated on the basis of fuel efficiency improvements on a model to model basis, but rather on the average fuel efficiency of all autos sold. As U.S. consumers buy more large cars, General Motors and Ford have sold more large cars. These two companies thus have fallen far short of the CAFE standards since 1984, despite the fact that their models are more fuel efficient. As a result, they face nearly $1 billion in fines. They would have to lay off huge numbers of workers from factories producing full-size models to meet CAFE standards.

It is ironic that the auto industry's success in producing fuel efficient large cars threatens crushing action by the government. Former Secretary of Transportation Elizabeth Dole responded by granting temporary reprieves to GM and Ford. The U.S. auto industry can begin regaining its competitive edge at home and abroad if Washington abolishes the CAFE standards.

Plank 32. Decontrol natural gas prices fully.

Control of natural gas prices was partly responsible for the energy crisis in the 1970s. Artificially low prices gave little incentive for exploration of new energy sources when foreign oil supplies were interrupted. In the late 1970s, natural gas prices were partially decontrolled. But, although newly discovered gas could be sold at phased-in market prices, gas from old oil fields is still subject to controls. Critics of even this limited decontrol predicted sharp price rises. But they overlooked the fact that decontrol encouraged more exploration and thus more supplies, keeping prices down. There is no valid economic reason for continued gas price controls. Natural gas price controls should be ended as soon as possible.

Plank 33. Shift the emphasis of safety regulation from safety standards based on specific equipment to standards based on results.

The 1970 Occupational Safety and Health Act (OSHA) regulates activities in the workplace to promote employee health and safety. Yet OSHA regulations that specify particular safety equipment or procedures often burden firms with unnecessary costs because cheaper methods of securing the same or even a greater degree of safety are available but do not fit the regulations.

Example: OSHA tends to prefer to promote safety through structural or equipment changes in the workplace rather than simple, and less costly, changes in procedures or clothing. Thus, rather than allowing cheap yet effective disposable face masks as a means of protecting employees against cotton dust, OSHA requires expensive changes in the machines that produce the dust. High noise levels are often dealt with through similar changes in machines rather than through far less costly ear plugs.

The goal of OSHA should be to promote safe working environments, not to mandate particular technologies. Unnecessarily expensive methods of assuring worker safety add to the costs of doing business and make American firms less competitive. If standards were based on results, and businesses given the freedom to choose the

73

best way to obtain the required result, workplace safety would improve and the costs to businesses would be reduced. OSHA's mandate should be changed to allow the maximum amount of flexibility in applying safety standards to achieve the maximum amount of safety.

Plank 34. Require "Job and Competitiveness Impact Statements" for new government rules and regulations.

In the past, legislators and administrators have paid too little attention to the potentially adverse impact of regulations on the ability of U.S. companies to compete with foreign rivals and to create new jobs. Often government regulations add substantially to the costs of doing business while yielding little in the way of public good, or providing benefits at a cost much higher than necessary. In addition, the uncertainty created by ever-changing federal regulations makes it difficult for businesses to plan ahead and invest in new products and enterprises. This weakens the U.S. economy.

Congress and the Executive Branch should require a "Job and Competitiveness Impact Statement" for new rules and regulations applied to business. This function could be handled by the Office of Management and Budget and the Congressional Budget Office. Such a statement should indicate: 1) how a proposed regulation might add to business overhead; 2) how smaller businesses might suffer disproportionately; 3) how entrepreneurs might be deterred from entering the market; and 4) how new hiring might be discouraged and layoffs encouraged.

— Judicial/Legal Reform —

Plank 35. Modify the merger restrictions in Section 7 of the Clayton Act.

Section 7 of the Clayton Act of 1914 bars mergers between companies in which the effect is "substantially to lessen competition, or tend to create a monopoly." This statute long has been enforced by the courts to prohibit any merger which increased concentration, regardless of whether the new firm would lessen effective competition, be more efficient or reduce prices to consumers. Big was considered bad, regardless of economic benefits.

Section 7 must be modernized. The Reagan Administration has proposed some legitimate changes. First, they would require that there be a "significant probability" that a merger would be competitively harmful before it could be prohibited. Second, anti-competitive mergers

75

would be defined as only those which increase the ability of firms to raise prices above competitive levels. Third, the changes would direct courts to consider important factors such as the ease of entry into the industry by new firms, the nature of the product, and potential efficiencies to be gained. These proposals would go a long way toward improving the merger laws.

Plank 36. Prohibit anti-merger lawsuits by competitors.

A common abuse of antitrust laws is through lawsuits filed by competing firms seeking to stop their rivals from becoming more competitive. This situation is particularly egregious in the case of mergers.

The focus of merger laws should be protecting consumers, not protecting firms from increased competition. Since a firm would not be likely to file suit to block a merger which would increase its own industry's prices, there is no good reason to allow such suits in the first place. Indeed, such suits are used to prevent many mergers which would be beneficial to consumers. Firms should thus be prohibited from suing to prevent mergers among their rivals.

Plank 37. Abolish automatic treble damages rules.

In most antitrust cases, a successful plaintiff is entitled to receive from the defendant a judgment three times the actual amount of damage suffered. The original purpose of such treble damages was to encourage meritorious antitrust claims and to discourage businesses from violating the antitrust laws. What has happened is that this has encouraged the filing of meritless claims in the hope of hitting the treble damages jackpot.

Faced with such suits, defendants often opt for large out-of-court settlements to avoid the risk of an unfavorable judgment. Worse, the prospect of treble damages has discouraged firms from engaging in many productive and efficient business activities, simply because of the possibility of litigation. This puts U.S. industry at a disadvantage to foreign firms, which are not so constrained. To resolve this problem, antitrust awards should be limited to the actual amount of damage suffered. Alternatively, as has been proposed by the Reagan Administration, the treble damages rule could be limited to only actual price-fixing cases.

Plank 38. Set reasonable standards for product liability suits.

In recent decades, the scope of product liability law has increased enormously, to the detriment of U.S. businesses and consumers. Not only have soaring liability costs boosted the prices that Americans pay for manufactured goods, but in some cases have prompted firms to stop marketing certain products, including valuable medicines. This hurts U.S. consumers, in addition to putting U.S. manufacturers at a disadvantage.

While manufacturers of course should be held liable for injuries caused by unreasonably dangerous products, the current system too often holds them liable in cases where the injury was due to the plaintiff's own negligence, or where the manufacturer could do nothing to make the product safer.

For the most part, liability law is a matter of state law, and the federal government should do nothing to interfere. In product liability, however, state legislators have had little incentive to reform their laws, since the benefits would be mostly dispersed to manufacturers outside their particular state. Thus national legislation setting

78

reasonable standards for the liability of manufacturers is desirable and necessary.

— Revise Federal Programs —

Plank 39. Reform unemployment insurance to reward displaced workers who find new jobs quickly.

Unemployed workers produce nothing. This impairs growth of the Gross National Product, reducing U.S. competitiveness. Unemployment compensation provides approximately 50 percent of a displaced worker's former wages for 26 weeks while he or she seeks new employment. Workers who obtain new jobs before their benefits run out, however, are sometimes tempted to wait until the end of the 26 week period so that they can collect all the payments to which they are entitled. To discourage this, unemployment insurance should be reformed to reward displaced workers who find new jobs quickly.

Under the current system, unemployed workers receive equal payments every week. This gives workers no greater incentive to return to work on the tenth or even twentieth week of unemployment than on the third week. Instead of this, the compensation could be "front-end loaded," providing the largest payment the first week of unemployment and scaling it downward until it was zero at the end of the period during which it was paid. The same total amount of compensation would still be available to the worker if he or she remained unemployed for the entire 26 weeks. Yet the unemployed worker would have greater incentive to find new work quickly.

— Protect America's — Competitive Secrets

Plank 40. Tighten the Freedom of Information Act to ensure the confidentiality of U.S. trade secrets.

The Freedom of Information Act (FOIA) of 1974 is to ensure citizens access to information about themselves that the federal government may have. In the past dozen years, however, those who mainly avail themselves of the FOIA have not been private citizens or even public interest groups or journalists. Rather, FOIA has been used chiefly by businesses, including many foreign companies, seeking the trade secrets of other firms. Businesses dealing with the federal government or attempting to comply with federal regulations are often required to disclose proprietary information to the government. Other companies seek — and can obtain — such information via the FOIA. This not only violates basic property rights, but allows foreign firms to compete unfairly with the U.S.

This problem can be resolved in part by taking three important steps. First, restrict the types of information government agencies can demand from firms. Second, restrict the types of information government agencies can release without a court order. And third, give firms providing information the right to charge for information released by government agencies.

Plank 41. Strengthen international agreements affecting "intellectual property rights."

Property rights are at the basis of a free market system. Protecting intellectual property, such as patents and trademarks, is one of government's most important functions. When foreign companies can steal and use U.S. patents, they are often able to produce lower-priced goods simply because they do not have to recover research and development costs. And by counterfeiting U.S. trademarked goods, foreign firms can exploit advertising and marketing paid for by American firms. The Reagan Administration correctly has made the protection of

81

property rights of U.S. companies a central goal of its international policy.

It is difficult to deal with this problem when foreign counterfeiters are selling overseas. When counterfeit goods enter the U.S., however, the U.S. International Trade Commission (ITC) can take steps to deal with them. For example, it can prohibit certain imports or require payments from the counterfeiter to the patent holder. Yet ITC policy seems confused. Sometimes the ITC requires that a U.S. company prove not only that its patent has been stolen but also that its business is adversely affected by the import of illegally produced goods. Such an "injury test" is inappropriate; the issue is property rights. If an unscrupulous author took another man's published work, replaced the true author's name with his own, published it, and tried to market it as his own work, the case would clearly be one of theft. No one would ask about the effects of the plagiarized work on the sales of the original.

The protection of U.S. firms in cases of patent and trademark theft is an important function of the ITC. Section 337 should be amended to make clear that an injury test is not required and that theft alone is grounds for relief against a foreign country.

STRATEGY

Competitiveness has become a Washington buzzword. Unfortunately, the definition of this term is not very clear. Even those who favor an increased state role in the economy wrap themselves in the competitiveness mantle. Some advocate "national industrial planning," that is, federal determination of what is to be produced in the U.S., in what quantities, and to be sold at what prices. Trade protectionism is offered to "protect" U.S. jobs. But, in fact, wherever such nationalist socialist schemes have been tried in the world, they have been abject failures.

A competitive economy offers the American people maximum economic prosperity and freedom of choice. Thus, any reforms to aid U.S. competitiveness must be judged in terms of three questions based on fundamental economic goals: 1) Does the policy increase the nation's standard of living; 2) Does the policy increase consumer choice and reduce the costs of goods and services; and 3) Does the policy expand employment opportunities? These three components of a competitive economy are best achieved through increasing economic productivity. Productivity is best promoted by policies that encourage economic flexibility.

83

OBSTACLES

Foremost among roadblocks to a competitive economy are the special interest groups that benefit from government subsidies, favors, and trade protection. Less efficient industries and unions representing these sectors often seek favors from government that harm America's overall competitive status. For example, when inefficient steel producers receive trade protection, American manufacturers using steel, such as auto companies or producers of farm equipment, suffer.

Another obstacle to reform are bureaucrats whose jobs are tied to the continuation of economically harmful policies and regulations. Government employees have little incentive to eliminate their own regulatory functions even when these functions are economically counterproductive or could be performed better with less government resources.

A third obstacle to restoring America's competitiveness is elected officials who make short-sighted appeals to vested interests with additional government programs and controls. Additional government regulations give the impression that perceived problems are being "solved" when, in fact, the economy in general suffers more in the long run. Finally, because the term "competitiveness" is often ill defined, some alleged reforms harm America's competitive status. Many see

84

competitiveness as the ability of some given industry in the U.S. to do well against foreign competitors. Perhaps the most serious misperception is the belief that to be competitive, the U.S. must "win" in an international competition against other countries that "lose." In fact, world economic prosperity is best achieved when all countries grow.

TACTICS

Expose Protectionist Schemes Carrying "Competitiveness" Labels. *Most bad policies advocated in the name of competitiveness stem from a failure to define the economic goals that a policy should seek. When all of the implications of such policies are examined, they usually are found to create more economic harm than good or to aid narrow interest groups at the expense of the public. Proponents of a competitive economy should measure all proposals by three criteria:*

1) Does the policy increase the nation's standard of living and economic growth? Some opponents of the free market would make all Americans poorer and hold down economic expansion with protectionist trade policies, all in the name of some ill-defined conception of national economic "strength." High standards of living for all Americans should be the goal of all economic policy.

85

2) Does the policy increase consumer choice and reduce the costs of goods and services? Ultimately, in a free market system, the consumer rules. Any policy that diminishes consumer choice should be rejected.

3) Does the competitiveness policy expand employment opportunities? Trade protectionism or subsidies to industries meant to preserve jobs in one sector of the economy usually create more unemployment in other sectors. High real wages in the U.S. are the result of high productivity, the sign of a competitive economy.

Stress Productivity. *High standards of living, maximum consumer choice, and expanded job opportunities, the three components of a competitive economy, are best achieved through ever increasing economic productivity. Industries that grow more productive turn out more goods and services for less resources. This means a genuine increase in real wealth, not a stealing of resources by the government from one special interest group to benefit another.*

Emphasize Flexibility. *Productivity is best promoted by economic flexibility. To be competitive with other countries, the American system must retain the maximum economic flexibility to permit the factors of production to be redistributed quickly and efficiently from less valued to higher valued economic functions. Economic flexibility requires the removal or revision of many government controls*

86

*and regulations. Such controls add to the costs of produc-
tion and send businessmen looking for tax shelters, government favors, and quick profits at the expense of long-term
productivity improvements, all to counter the effects of such
controls.*

**Highlight How Government Policies Harm America's
Competitiveness.** *When the costs of government policies
are highlighted simply and effectively, the virtues of less
regulation become clear. Thus, when it is pointed out that
70 percent of U.S. goods are subject to foreign competition,
it is clear why antitrust laws that prohibit American businesses from cooperating to battle the imports is an anti-competitive policy. When it is noted that Americans pay $5
billion annually in higher costs for autos and $26 billion per
year more in increased prices for textile and apparel
products, it becomes clear why trade protection makes
America poor.*

COALITION FOR VICTORY

Consumers. *Anti-competitive policies such as trade protectionism and excessive regulation of businesses add directly
to the costs of consumer products. In the past, many consumer organizations have failed to highlight adequately the
need for pro-competitive reforms. Consumers should play
an important role in a competitiveness coalition.*

87

New, Expanding Industries. *New, expanding industries such as high tech firms are ill served by increased government regulations or protectionism. Such businesses are crucial to a competitive economy. They provide the new products and innovations that keep the U.S. at the world's economic cutting edge. Such new businesses are generally risky. Excessive government regulations can prevent them from getting off the ground. Attempts by the government to target such businesses with special favors are equally destructive. There is no indication that government bureaucrats know better than entrepreneurs which businesses will succeed or fail. If governments make such choices and are wrong, potentially successful firms could be destroyed. New, expanding industries thus have good reason to favor pro-competitive reforms.*

Workers. *Many workers mistakenly see government regulation and trade protection as being in their economic interest. In fact, such policies at best benefit limited groups for short periods of time while leading to a long-term fall in living standards and real purchasing power. In a productive economy, a worker's labor produces more and thus is worth more to the owners and management of businesses. A worker can "trade" his labor for greater purchasing power. And in a productive society, labor is in great demand. Profitable job opportunities abound. Workers therefore have a long-term interest in an economically flexible, productive economy.*

Trade Sensitive Sectors. *Sectors that depend heavily on exports and imports, and many that face import competition, would benefit from pro-competitive economic reforms. Trade protection in the U.S. means fewer dollars overseas to purchase American goods and means that trade barriers would rise against U.S. exports. Thus American farmers and aircraft manufacturers find their overseas sales harmed by U.S. trade barriers. Trade protection also harms import dependent industries such as retailers, dock workers, and truckers. Finally, industries subject to foreign competition have a stake in less government regulation. Environmental laws, for example, impose high costs on U.S. businesses and make them less able to compete with foreign firms not subject to such regulations. When American firms are prohibited by antitrust laws from cooperating, while foreign governments encourage their own businesses to work together, U.S. enterprises are at a disadvantage.*

Chapter Five

Trade

International trade is a vital component of a strong and prosperous economy. A high level of international trade means jobs in U.S. export industries, and a wider choice and more competitive prices for American consumers. While protectionism may help some individual workers and some factory owners, it is at enormous cost to most American workers and consumers. And, as the aftermath of the 1929 stock market crash demonstrates, attempts by one country to gain short-term benefits for some of its domestic industries through protectionism can turn quickly into a trade war which drags down the economies of all industrialized countries.

To foster freer international trade, the U.S. needs to adopt a two-pronged approach. First, steps should be taken to remove federal government-inflicted barriers to American exports and obstacles to foreign imports. These rules benefit small but powerful groups at the expense of millions of Americans. Second, there needs to be a "build down" in restrictive trade practices around the world. This would allow U.S. businesses to sell more goods overseas and help improve the standard of living in the recipient countries.

— Fight Protectionism —

Plank 42. Require the Congressional Budget Office to issue regular statistics on the costs of U.S. trade protectionism to consumers and businesses.

The Congressional Budget Office (CBO) provides valuable analyses of the effects of various proposed congressional actions. Yet the effects of trade legislation are rarely examined by CBO even though the impact of such laws can be devastating economically. Example: estimates by private research firms as well as by the President's Council of Economic Advisors find that proposed congressional limits on textile imports would cost American consumers tens of billions of dollars in higher prices. Each $15,000 per year textile job saved, moreover, would come at a cost of hundreds of thousands of dollars. Other private studies have shown that trade restrictions on steel costs

U.S. manufacturers of such products as automobiles and farm equipment over $3 billion in higher costs.

CBO should regularly report on the effects of proposed trade legislation so that Congress might avoid actions that could be harmful to the U.S. economy.

Plank 43. Remove barriers to the development and export of natural gas from Alaska's North Slope.

The U.S. government prohibits the export of natural gas from Alaska's North Slope. These restrictions were meant to preserve U.S. energy resources when it was believed there was a worldwide energy shortage. Currently Alaskan natural gas is not used in the U.S. It is pumped back into the oil wells from which it comes as a natural result of oil extraction. This replacement process loses part of the gas and in the long run will damage the oil fields.

Restrictions on the sale of Alaskan natural gas to Japan and other nations should be lifted. Since this gas is not being used by Americans, it would not have to be replaced by imports. Such sales to Japan could total $6.5 billion annually.

Plank 44. Allow the export of raw timber harvested on public lands.

Alleging a timber shortage, various interest groups in 1968 prodded Congress into banning the export of raw cut timber from U.S. public lands. These lands contain well over half the U.S. timber stock. Companies owning private forests also are not allowed to replace logs they export overseas with logs purchased from public lands.

The fact is, there is no timber shortage. The U.S. has more forest land today than it had at the turn of the century. By contrast, Japan suffers a severe shortage of timber. Lifting the prohibition on exports of timber harvested on U.S. public lands could generate $1 billion annually in export sales to Japan.

Plank 45. Change cargo preference rules that raise the prices of U.S. agricultural exports.

Cargo preference laws require half of U.S. government-financed agricultural products for export to be shipped on U.S. vessels. These laws are little more than special interest legislation to benefit the shipping industry at the expense of farmers. With U.S. agricultural exports falling from $43.8 billion in 1981 to only $26.6 billion in 1986, farmers cannot afford to use overpriced American shipping.

The U.S. Agriculture Department estimates that cargo preference adds about $35 per metric ton to U.S. farm exports. A recent U.S. District Court ruling on cargo preferences, moreover, could add up to 15 percent extra to the costs of such exported goods as wheat and soybeans. This, of course, would discourage foreign purchases. To make U.S. agricultural products more competitive in world markets, such cargo preference restrictions should be removed.

Plank 46. Remove "voluntary" quota restrictions and dismantle U.S.-enforced cartels that restrict supplies of goods and raw materials in the U.S.

Under so-called voluntary restraint agreements, foreign governments agree to limit the amount of a particular good that their businesses ship to America. In addition to quota limits, cartels invoke government-mandated production limits to keep prices above market levels.

Quotas and cartels add tens of billions of dollars to the cost of such consumer goods as automobiles and clothing. In addition, they harm many U.S. manufacturers and exporters, such as makers of farm equipment or automobiles, which are now less competitive because they are forced to purchase higher-priced and sometimes lower quality U.S. steel.

— Encourage Free Trade — Worldwide

Plank 47. Participate in the Uruguay Round of the General Agreement on Tariffs and Trade and reject legislation violating this agreement.

After World War II, the world's non-communist countries came together to promote prosperity and freer trade through the General Agreements on Tariffs and Trade (GATT). In numerous subsequent rounds of negotiations, tariffs have been lowered substantially. In a round that began at U.S. insistence in Uruguay in 1986, topics such as trade in services, licensing restrictions, and government subsidies are being considered. These are areas of particular interest to the U.S.: services are becoming an increasingly important source of American export earnings; licensing restrictions not only hurt sales of U.S. products already on the market but can keep new products out of foreign markets as well; and unfair foreign government subsidies to businesses distort the world market and make it difficult for U.S. firms to compete.

The Administration's authority to negotiate in the current GATT round expired at the beginning of 1988. The trade bill before Congress, meanwhile, contains many provisions that violate the GATT. Passage of such measures would undermine GATT efforts to open markets. To assure America's continuing participation in these trade liberalization talks, Congress should renew the Administration's negotiating authority and avoid legislation that violates the GATT.

Plank 48. Begin negotiations to phase out all agricultural trade barriers and subsidies.

The federal government sets price floors above the actual market price for farm commodities. If prices fall below these levels, the government purchases commodities from farmers. Overproduction thus is encouraged and the market becomes glutted. Yet the price floors result in high export prices, making U.S. farmers uncompetitive in the world market.

In 1986, these subsidies cost the U.S. taxpayer $26 billion. The European Community (EC) spends approximately the same amount to subsidize its farmers. Much of the EC surplus is dumped on the world market at low subsidized prices, making it even more difficult for American farmers to sell their products overseas. The EC and most other countries maintain trade barriers to agricultural goods, further hurting the U.S. farmer.

The U.S. should negotiate with the European Community and in the Uruguay round of the General Agreement on Tariffs and Trade talks to eliminate all subsidies and trade barriers to agricultural products.

Plank 49. Create Free Trade Areas with countries that seek totally open markets.

If two countries desire completely free trade with each other, they can establish a Free Trade Area (FTA). Through FTAs, both countries would remove substantially all tariff and non-tariff barriers. An FTA is by definition "fair" since both countries open their markets to each other on a reciprocal basis. FTAs also put pressure on third countries to open their markets. If, for instance, the U.S. and Japan both were selling a certain product in a country with which the U.S. had an FTA, the Japanese products would be subject to tariffs while the American goods would not. This would place the Japanese goods at a disadvantage, creating an incentive for Japan to seek better trade terms.

The U.S. currently is phasing in an FTA with Israel. An FTA with Canada now awaits approval by the U.S. Congress and the Canadian Parliament. Other countries have expressed interest in FTAs with the U.S. including Singapore, Thailand, the Republic of China on Taiwan, Uruguay, and Iceland. The U.S. should negotiate FTAs with any country or group of countries that desires completely free trade.

✳　　✳　　✳

STRATEGY

America's trade deficit should be reduced by expanding exports, not restricting imports. America's trade deficit is a symptom of policies which made America less flexible, less innovative, and less competitive than other countries. Retreating into a protectionist shell will aggravate the problem and result in fewer jobs and lower incomes. History teaches that, at best, protectionism guarantees that America will decay slowly. At worst, protectionism will trigger retalia-

tion from other countries, a contraction in world markets and ultimately, a depression — as occurred in the 1930s due in large part to an American-initiated trade war.

The lines between free trade and protectionist policies are clearly drawn. On the one hand, forces in Congress and several presidential aspirants continue to advocate restrictive trade policies. On Capitol Hill, for example, the protectionist Omnibus Trade Bill is working its way through conference committees to a final vote in both Houses. On the other hand, free trade advocates are supporting the historic Free Trade Agreement between the U.S. and Canada.

OBSTACLES

A group of vested interests seeks to preserve the monopoly privileges that trade restrictions grant them at the expense of the American worker and consumer. Among the most powerful is organized labor. To protect their power, union leaders wage an all-out campaign to "preserve" jobs in inefficient industries no matter what the cost to consumers or American workers in the long run. Example: the steel unions successfully drove up wages in the 1970s, leading to increased production costs and reduced capital for modernization. As a result, the enfeebled American steel industry has been at a competitive disadvantage against foreign steel firms. Hundreds of thousands of workers lost their jobs.

100

Another obstacle to change is inefficient, but politically powerful industries. Traditional industries such as steel, autos, and textiles have a vested interest in protectionism. To make matters worse, protectionism gives politicians an issue with a clearly defined constituency, and an easy means of demonstrating "compassion" for American workers and contempt for foreigners who, after all, do not vote in U.S. elections. It also provides powerful rhetoric such as "level playing field" and "fair trade."

TACTICS

Identify Protectionism's Costs and Free Trade's Benefits. *Industries and groups of individuals hurt by protectionism or who will benefit from freer trade must be mobilized through a better understanding of the ways in which trade policies directly affect them. Plank 42 requires the federal government to issue regular statistics on the cost of protectionism. Congress must recognize that there are significant constituencies adversely affected by restrictive trade policies. The groups must be prepared to communicate their concerns directly to Congress.*

Mobilize the Consumer Lobby. *Consumer advocates should be encouraged to marshall their forces in support of free trade. A coalition of consumer groups should be formed to fight for the consumer's right to free trade. A list of free* *trade policy objectives should be drafted and pursued vigorously by the coalition through public and voter identification and grass roots campaigns. Other organizations and individuals who benefit from free trade should be brought into the coalition, including farmers, retailers and other business sectors.*

Show How Protectionism Costs Jobs. *Supporters of free trade must point out how protectionism will cost American workers their jobs. Protecting jobs and profits in one industry locks labor and capital into inefficient industries, stifling job creation in healthy industries and reducing incentives for firms to modernize and respond to changing technology and consumer demand. Example: A 1986 study by the International Business and Economic Research Corporation reports that a House protectionism bill designed to "save" 20,627 textile jobs would cost 20,373 retail jobs. The net gain of 254 jobs was to cost American consumers more than $4 million per job. Thirty-five states would suffer a net loss of jobs under the bill, with midwestern states losing 15,555 jobs for every 4,043 "saved" and mountain states losing 3,454 for every 433 "saved."*

Make Free Trade Agreements a Key Political Issue. *The recent Free Trade Agreement (FTA) between the U.S. and Canada should serve as a springboard for generating public support for similar agreements with other countries. As Congress considers the U.S.-Canada accord in early 1988,* *the political lines should be drawn clearly between free traders and protectionists — between reactionary protectors of small, politically powerful interests who are selfishly denying new economic opportunities to Americans and progressives seeking true, fair, and free trade rather than self-destructive market restrictions. Candidates for political office should be asked where they stand on the agreement.*

COALITION FOR VICTORY

Consumers. *Trade is the number one consumer issue. Protectionism costs an American family of four between $1,500 and $2,000 annually in higher prices, more than most families pay in taxes. Consumers pay $5 billion more for cars each year, $26 billion more for textiles, and $1 billion extra for shoes because of protectionism. America's poor, and those on fixed incomes such as families and the elderly, suffer most from higher prices due to protectionism.*

Trade Dependent Industries. *Industries that compete efficiently in world markets are penalized by protectionism, which gives special advantages to their inefficient competitors. Moreover, export sensitive industries such as agriculture and shipping are devastated by restrictive trade policies. Retailers, who import many products, also have much to lose by protectionist policies which drive up prices, but not profits. American farm machinery manufacturers, cut off from cheap and adequate supplies of foreign steel, see*

103

their costs increase, making them less able to export their products.

Advocates of Third World Development. *Many public service interest groups (liberal and conservative) and various agencies in the U.S. government correctly are concerned about continuing poverty in the Third World. Export-related jobs offer opportunities of upward mobility for the poor in developing nations. Exports represent the most thriving sectors of many Third World economies. For the economies of such countries to grow, the U.S. market must remain open to their goods. American protectionism would doom many of these countries to continuing poverty and misery. And, of course, poverty stricken countries cannot afford to purchase U.S. goods. Groups and agencies seeking economic growth in the Third World should be brought into a free trade coalition.*

Chapter Six

International Economic Development

Strong economic growth in developing countries — formally known as Less Developed Countries or LDCs — is good for the U.S. as well as for the citizens of those countries. Experience teaches that the best recipe for growth is indigenous free enterprise, not socialist-style central planning or bureaucratized "help" from the Western planners of the multinational lending agencies.

To spur economic growth in LDCs, the U.S. should ensure that its programs and actions encourage widely based free enterprise. First, U.S. bilateral aid or assistance through international organizations to LDCs should be linked to free market reforms, including lower taxes, less regulation, and the privatization of state industries. Second, debt repayment should be encouraged not by a debilitating and ineffective strategy of austerity, which has

105

provoked hostility towards the U.S. and reduces the capacity of countries to make repayments, but rather by encouraging growth and by introducing such positive innovations as "debt-for-equity" swaps. Third, LDC economies should be stimulated by opening U.S. markets further to LDC products and by fighting protectionism. And fourth, there should be pressure on the World Bank and International Monetary Fund, and action within the U.S. Agency for International Development, to end loans that foster centralization and "crony capitalism" in LDCs.

Plank 50. Promote growth-oriented economic policies in developing countries by linking U.S. aid to deregulation, tax reform, and privatization.

The Third World's economic problems, for the most part, are self-imposed. They are the result of strict government regulation of the economy and state ownership of major industries. For decades wages, prices, banking, credit, production, distribution, and trade have been directed by powerful bureaucrats, politicians, and vested interest groups with close government ties. LDCs have been getting away with their devastating economic policies because they receive billions of dollars in aid from the U.S. Treasury to finance the operating deficits of inefficient state firms.

It is time for U.S. foreign aid to be linked to the elimination of anti-growth policies. The U.S. Agency for International Development (AID) correctly has begun a number of "policy dialogues" in LDCs. These are aimed at achieving deregulation, exchange rate reform, and the privatization of money-losing state enterprises. Yet while these dialogues continue, many countries persist with self-destructive economic policies. Examples: Peru continues to receive U.S. foreign aid, although its president recently nationalized the last of the banks in the private sector; Tanzania continues to receive such U.S. aid although it recently outlawed private trade in export crops, telling farmers to sell to the government at set prices or not at all. Subsidization of such policies with U.S. taxpayers' funds must end.

Plank 51. Promote debt-for-equity swaps to ease Third World debt and spur reforms.

The Third World is now saddled with an estimated trillion dollars in foreign debt. Its capital flight problem continues to bleed it of badly needed hard currency. From 1983 to 1985, while Latin America's top ten debtors borrowed $44 billion abroad, their own citizens transferred $31 billion out of the region. Today, many U.S. banks understandably are increasingly unwilling to lend these heavy debtors further funds.

Debt-for-equity swaps are one way to deal with this problem. In a swap, a foreign investor or native of the debtor country buys debt notes with U.S. dollars at their prevailing market discount from the creditor bank and presents them to the government of the debtor country for local currency. This currency in turn often is used to acquire an enterprise or to fund plant expansion.

More than $5 billion in developing country foreign debt has been retired in this manner. Chile, with the best crafted and most attractive swap regulations, already has retired about $2 billion of its foreign debt through debt-for-equity swaps. Currently, only about half of the fifteen top debtor countries allow swaps. Fewer still allow their own citizens to participate in them, thereby missing an important opportunity to recapture capital which has fled their countries. Swaps, meanwhile, force governments to take a hard look at changes in their investment climates — such as their exchange rate policies, foreign ownership rules, repatriation of capital and profits, labor regulations, and even corruption. U.S. bilateral aid, as well as assistance from the World Bank and IMF, should be made conditional upon debtor countries allowing debt-for-equity swaps.

Plank 52. Promote employee stock ownership plans in LDCs as a means to privatize state-owned industries and widen capital ownership.

Bloated and inefficient state-owned firms are a leading cause of budget deficits and government borrowing in the Third World. While governments often oppose privatization of these enterprises due to strong worker opposition, privatization through employee stock ownership plans (ESOPs) could win worker backing and could turn money-losing companies into profitable ventures.

Under such plans, workers purchase or are given shares in a company. In the U.S., for example, the West Virginia-based Weirton Steel Company, once on the brink of bankruptcy, was acquired by its employees in 1982 through an ESOP. The company is now posting record profits while much of the U.S. steel industry stagnates. In Britain, one of Prime Minister Margaret Thatcher's most successful privatization plans was an ESOP — the sale of the National Freight Corporation, the country's largest trucking firm, to its workers. ESOPs strengthen workers' support for free enterprise and property rights.

Plank 53. Oppose new U.S. contributions to the International Monetary Fund, the World Bank, Inter-American Development Bank, and other multinational banks that encourage destructive economic policies.

The International Monetary Fund (IMF), World Bank, and Inter-American Development Bank (IDB) are among the multilateral institutions established to promote worldwide economic growth. Many of their activities, however, have been counterproductive. The IMF, for example, gives loans to Less Developed Countries (LDCs) to help cover foreign debts. While some of the conditions attached to these loans, such as cutting fiscal deficits, are correct, other IMF loan conditions necessitate such economically destructive policies as higher taxes and trade protectionism.

The World Bank loans money for development projects. Yet many of these projects are economically questionable. Some construct unnecessary roads or other infrastructure projects that provide make-work government jobs for facilities that are later underutilized. Other projects are environmentally damaging. Example: the "Polonoreste" project in Brazil devastated a tropical rain forest three-quarters the size of France. World Bank loans often sup-

110

port state-run or subsidized industries, rather than private market-oriented projects.

The IDB frequently distributes loans based on political considerations. Corrupt politicians in various Latin American countries survive on IDB funds. Banking procedures are sloppy, leading to serious abuses. Example: Nicaragua, whose IDB loans were cut off because of failure to pay on past loans, notified the IDB that it had deposited money in IDB accounts to cover some of these debts. The IDB, without verifying these deposits, released new money to the Sandinistas. The Sandinistas, however, had lied about the deposits. They "round-tripped" the funds, using the new money to pay off old loans.

U.S. contributions to these multilateral institutions often allow LDC governments to continue economically destructive policies which do little more than strengthen the power of privileged, ruling elites and their cronies. The U.S. contributes around 20 percent of the funds for the IMF and World Bank and over 34 percent of the funds for the IDB. In the past 40 years, the U.S. has contributed over $33 billion to these banks. This year, the World Bank will seek as much as $75 billion in new cash, lending authority, and loan guarantees. The other institutions also periodically request more funds. In light of their dismal records, they deserve no more U.S. taxpayers' dollars to carry out their destructive economic policies.

111

Plank 54. Strengthen the Caribbean Basin Initiative by eliminating existing trade restrictions.

The 1983 Caribbean Basin Initiative (CBI) aims to spur economic development by providing easier access for Caribbean goods to the U.S. market. The CBI, however, maintains trade restrictions on many of the products in which the CBI countries are competitive. Examples: frozen orange juice, beef, petroleum products, and textiles.

The CBI has suffered various setbacks. Among the most serious is the 65 percent cut since 1985 in the quotas of sugar which the CBI countries can export to the U.S. Sugar is the main crop and principal export of many CBI countries.

The U.S. at least should totally restore the CBI sugar quotas. In the long term, Congress should phase out the U.S. price support program for sugar entirely and should open the U.S. market to more imports from non-subsidized producers. In addition, the U.S. should continue to oppose European agricultural subsidies, which have resulted in massive dumping and the distortion of sugar prices on the world market. Finally, the U.S. should

112

remove trade restrictions on such products as beef and petroleum from Caribbean nations.

Plank 55. Oppose the admission of the Soviet Union to the International Monetary Fund (IMF), the World Bank, and the General Agreement on Tariffs and Trade (GATT).

The goals of the IMF, World Bank, and GATT include promoting worldwide economic growth, especially in the Third World, and free trade. IMF and World Bank policies, in fact, often have been counterproductive. The Reagan Administration is attempting to move these organizations in a more free market direction. Further, the U.S. is negotiating trade liberalization in the GATT.

Increasingly, there are indications that the USSR wants to join these organizations. Yet the Kremlin's economic philosophy remains completely contrary to the free market goals that the U.S. is promoting. The Soviets could be expected to undermine these important efforts. Instead, Soviet membership could funnel U.S. funds to Marxist economies, perpetuating regimes that offer no hope for individual freedom and economic opportunity. The U.S. should oppose Soviet membership in the organizations until Moscow initiates sweeping economic and human rights reforms and cease its expansionist foreign policy.

✱   ✱   ✱

STRATEGY

L*DC poverty is an economic and security problem for the U.S. LDC poverty, moreover, is rooted in socialist economic policies. Economic growth, prosperity, human dignity, and peace can be achieved only through market-oriented reforms in LDCs that free the people to work and benefit from their efforts. The Third World debt crisis continues unrelieved by current policies. Billions of dollars in foreign aid funds and new bank loans have gone to LDC countries in the last few years. Yet real market-oriented economic reforms are nowhere in sight. Instead, the World Bank seeks $65 billion to $75 billion in new funds for such countries, part of this to come out of the pockets of the American taxpayers.*

OBSTACLES

Four identifiable groups oppose policies offering a free market approach to lesser developed countries. First, a number of large American banks are nervous about any policies that may endanger repayment of foreign debts. In particular, banks holding large debts of LDCs would view cutting off U.S. aid to those countries as a threat to debt payments. Second, a small but powerful group of domestic industries and lobbyists views exports from LDCs as a threat to its existence. The sugar lobby, for instance, opposes liberalization of America's protectionist sugar import policy and favors legislation to protect U.S. sugar producers. And textiles and steel resist a pro-growth import policy for LDCs.

Third, bureaucrats and politicians within LDCs resist privatization and free market approaches for a variety of reasons. Anti-Americanism and socialistic sentiment motivate some of these opponents, while others simply resist changes which threaten their privileged posts. Finally, bureaucrats within U.S. and international development agencies often resist market oriented reforms that could threaten their own jobs and influence in LDCs. Market reforms, once put in place, usually eliminate the need for foreign aid and for bureaucrats administering such programs.

TACTICS

Emphasize the Economic and Security Benefits of LDC Development. *LDC economic issues generally are low priority in American political discussions. Yet many "high profile" issues grow out of the economic failures of the Third World. Political leaders must stress the importance of LDC economic growth as a means to prevent long-term problems for the U.S. A prosperous nation, for example, is less subject to communist subversion. Economic misery in under-developed countries can encourage support for Marxist guerrilla movements. To avoid the need to send U.S. troops to fight in Third World conflicts, economic development should be given priority. In addition, the U.S. has an economic reason to promote LDC growth. American banks and businesses have substantial investments in Third World countries. Strong economic growth is the best way to protect such investments. Prosperous economies, meanwhile, are better able to purchase U.S. goods and reduce America's trade deficit.*

Stress How Market-Oriented Reforms Help the Poor in the LDCs. *In LDCs, socialist-oriented policies are primarily responsible for continuing poverty, yet socialism ironically is often equated with compassion. True compassion, however, would spur effective policies to raise LDC masses from their poverty. At the heart of these policies are free*

116

market reforms. As was the case in the last century, those favoring economic freedom are the true progressives.

COALITION FOR VICTORY

Consumers. *Allowing people in LDCs to sell their products in the U.S. is one of the best ways to promote prosperity and free markets worldwide. In addition, American consumers will benefit enormously from the greater choice and lower prices of products produced by LDCs with expanding economies. America's poor and the elderly living on fixed incomes, in particular, will benefit from lower prices. Protectionism raises consumer prices. A pro-growth U.S. strategy for the LDCs should be designed as a major consumerist issue in the U.S. It should be supported by all organizations claiming to be working for consumer rights.*

Bankers. *Bankers should understand that unless LDCs grow and begin to produce quality products for the export market, they will not earn the foreign exchange to pay their foreign debt. American bankers should be encouraged to oppose the sugar and textile lobbies and other industries whose protectionist policies endanger LDC growth, which, in turn, endangers repayment of foreign debt. American banks therefore should pressure the U.S. government to promote policies in IMF, AID and elsewhere that spur growth.*

LDC Politicians. *Leaders of LDCs must be convinced of the political benefits to them of promoting market economic policies. Free market policies, for example, mean leaders can advocate economic growth rather than painful austerity. Through privatization, meanwhile, leaders of LDCs can espouse worker control and other populist ideals within a capitalistic framework. If LDC leaders continue to balk, Washington should make aid contingent on LDC countries introducing some free market elements into their economies.*

LDC Workers and Unions. *Privatization gives workers a stake in their employer's business. This is proving especially appealing in LDCs where workers traditionally have had little power. Workers in LDCs should be encouraged to call for privatization and free markets.*

Liberals. *Those American liberals who insist that poverty is the primary reason for unrest in LDCs should be willing, if they are sincere, to back strategies for LDC economic growth.*

Environmentalists. *The IMF and World Bank have financed ecologically disastrous projects in the Third World. Useless public works projects have knocked down thousands of square miles of forests, silted rivers, forced thousands of people from their homes, and increased disease. Environ-*

mental groups should be enlisted to reform World Bank and IMF development policies.

Chapter Seven

Transportation

Good transportation is essential for a growing economy. Federal policy in recent years, however, has spurred pork barrel transportation spending, regulations inhibiting innovation in transportation, and policy decisions divorced from adequate considerations of cost and benefit. To be sure, much has been done to deregulate airlines and trucking. But if America's transportation system is to foster continued expansion of the economy, rather than create bottlenecks, more must be done.

First, the deregulation of the airline, trucking, and rail industries must be defended strenuously and extended. Second, federal control of such important segments of transportation as the air traffic control system and Amtrak should be transferred to America's private sector. Third, the federal government should end its control of the private space transportation industry, so that enterprising American firms can compete vigorously on what is certain to be the next commercial frontier. And fourth, the federal role in transportation needs to be reformed to end its interference in interstate transportation, to reduce pork barrel spending, to shift responsibilities to lower levels of government, and to foster a greater degree of privatization in urban transportation.

—— REGULATION ——

Plank 56. Defend airline deregulation and extend market mechanisms to airports and airways.

The 1978 deregulation of the airline industry has lowered fares significantly and is enabling more Americans to fly than ever. The Brookings Institution estimates total savings to consumers from airline deregulation at nearly $11 billion per year since 1978. At the same time, air safety continues to improve — the air fatality rate in the nine years since deregulation has been almost 50 percent lower than in the nine years before deregulation. Nevertheless, deregulation has accomplished only half its job. While the airlines are deregulated, the nation's airports and airways remain under direct government ownership and control. These vital parts of the transportation infrastructure, insulated from market incentives, have not been able to keep up with the growth of air traffic in recent years. The result has been increasing delays and frustration for air travelers.

Resolving these problems requires application of market principles to airports and airways. One way to do this is to establish a rational pricing system for landing rights at major airports. Instead of charging planes the same amount at any time of the day, fees should be varied by peak and off-peak hours, to distribute demand throughout the day. Fees for private aircraft should be raised, so that they pay in full the costs they impose on the system. Alternatively, an auction system for landing slots could be established, in which each slot is given to the highest bidder, treating the right to land as a valuable property right. In this way, peak-hour slots can be apportioned to those who value them the most and waste of these valuable airport resources would be discouraged. The result would be decreased congestion and delays for air travellers.

Plank 57. Further deregulate trucking rates and routes at the state and federal levels.

Congress partially deregulated America's trucking industry with the Motor Carrier Act of 1980. Since then trucking rates have dropped, service has improved, and competition has increased. All of this benefits the U.S. economy and consumers by lowering the cost of goods. At the same time, trucking service to small communities has continued.

Now it is time to dismantle the regulatory apparatus remaining in place. Truckers are still required, for example, to file millions of pages of documents with the Interstate Commerce Commission (ICC) each year, costing the economy millions of dollars. Many states continue to regulate strictly the activities of truckers within their states, damaging their own economies and interstate commerce generally. To complete the job of deregulation, it is necessary to end the remaining ICC controls over the industry, sparing truckers the paperwork burden of gaining formal approval of their rates and routes, and lessening the chance of a return to full regulation. In today's deregulated environment these requirements serve no real purpose, while imposing significant costs on truckers.

Policymakers should resist efforts to re-regulate the industry through the antitrust laws. Currently, trucking companies are allowed to participate in "rate bureaus" which formulate "list" prices for trucking services. While these rate bureaus have been criticized as "price-fixing" arrangements, they actually have little or no effect on prices in the competitive trucking industry, and provide valuable information services to truckers. Such voluntary arrangements within the industry should continue to be permitted, leaving the market — rather than the government — to decide whether they are necessary.

Plank 58. Re-examine the "Jones Act."

While most modes of transportation in the U.S. have been fully or partially deregulated, little has been done to reduce the restrictions on the maritime industry. One of the most harmful restrictions is the "Jones Act," passed by Congress in 1920. The law prohibits ships not built and registered in the U.S. and manned by U.S. crews from serving routes between U.S. ports. While intended to protect U.S. shipping, the long-term effect has been to make U.S. shipping uncompetitive with other forms of transportation, as operators are forced to use more costly U.S. crews. The Act has not even served to protect domestic shipbuilders, as no self-propelled liner vessels have been built for the U.S. mainland trade since World War II.

The Administration and Congress should re-examine thoroughly the need for the "Jones Act," carefully weighing whether it is worth the cost it imposes on the U.S.

economy, and, if repeal is not possible, looking for ways to reduce its harmful effects.

– RESTORE MARKET FORCES –

Plank 59. Privatize the air traffic control system.

The air traffic control system is currently owned and operated by the federal government through the Federal Aviation Administration. As part of the federal bureaucracy, the system lacks the flexibility and incentive to respond quickly and effectively to consumer demands. The result has been an inability to deal with growing air traffic, leading to an increase in flight delays and passenger frustration. The current system hinders traffic control in several ways. The federal civil service system, for example, makes it difficult to reassign or alter the duties of air traffic controllers. The FAA, moreover, lacks the flexibility to adopt innovative solutions to management/labor problems. Technological improvement is burdened by complex federal procurement rules. Even adoption of new traffic rules is slowed, due to federal rule-making procedures.

The best way to remove the political and bureaucratic impediments hindering the air traffic system would be to reorganize the system as a private not-for-profit corporation. Such a corporation could be owned by the users of the system — airlines, pilots, and perhaps even air traffic controllers — giving it the incentive to meet the needs of those users best. This is not an untried idea. In fact, the first radio-based ATC system in the United States was operated by a private corporation jointly owned by the airlines. Today, Aeradio Ltd., a British corporation, provides a range of air traffic services throughout the world.

Such a reorganization would increase the quality of air traffic services, as the ATC system would gain the flexibility and incentives necessary to increase its efficiency. At the same time, the safety of the air travel system would be maintained, and probably improved. The owners of the system, as its users, would have powerful incentives to maintain safety. By taking the air traffic control system out of the hands of the federal bureaucracy and reorganizing it as a user-owned private corporation, policy makers can help relieve the problems of the congested air travel system, while preserving and improving its safety.

Plank 60. Privatize Amtrak's northeast corridor.

When the federal government created Amtrak in 1970, U.S. taxpayers were assured that the company would soon be a "self-sustaining corporation." Today, Amtrak consumes over $600 million in annual federal subsidies. To a great degree, these subsidies have continued because the question has usually been posed as a choice between rail service with subsidy or no rail service at all. There is a third choice: privatization of the system, or at least the heavily travelled Northeast Corridor between Washington, D.C. and Boston. This portion of Amtrak's system almost breaks even on its operating costs, although it does not earn enough to cover capital costs. Under creative and innovative private management, however, many experts believe that the corridor can turn a real profit, thus continuing (or improving) service while saving taxpayers' money.

To broaden support for privatization, ownership of the system could be granted to Amtrak's employees, management, and even its riders. For instance, 80 percent of the stock in the company could be given without charge to Amtrak's employees — both labor and management. The rest could be granted to frequent riders on the basis of the number of miles they have travelled. This would ensure that the new owners would have an interest in Amtrak's successful operation, while turning potential opponents of privatization into supporters.

– REFORMING THE FEDERAL – ROLE

Plank 61. End federal funding of the interstate highway system.

The original objective of federal financing of road building was to construct the interstate highway system. This was an appropriate federal role: since all U.S. citizens benefit from an interconnected national highway system, federal taxpayers should bear the burden of paying for it. But now the interstate highway system is over 97 percent complete. Most federal funds now go toward financing local roads, ramps, bridges, and whatever other parochial, pork barrel public works projects congressmen can pack on to highway funding measures.

The federal government should stop funding highways, and leave this field to state and local governments, which are more familiar with local needs. The federal gasoline tax dedicated to highway funding should be abolished, allowing the states to use this revenue source as they see fit.

Plank 62. End federal restrictions on state highway spending.

When Congress distributes federal highway money to the states it routinely imposes onerous federal mandates which inflate construction costs by as much as 20 percent. Congress ought not use scarce highway funds to pursue goals unrelated to transportation. Rather these funds should be used for the sole purpose of road building and repair.

Under current law, 10 percent of all highway construction contracts must be awarded to businesses owned by "socially and economically disadvantaged individuals." State highway officials have pleaded with Congress to end this minority business program, because it costs the states tens of millions of dollars annually. The program grants contracts without competitive bids to companies that are supposed to be minority controlled. In fact, many contracts have been awarded to firms that turned out to be "false fronts" and other contracts have been politically guided. Even past supporters of the program acknowledge its failure. *The Washington Post*, on January 11,

1988, editorialized: "If it can't be fixed, and pretty fast, we say junk it. As it stands, the program does a disservice to the cause it's meant to help."

The minority set-aside programs should be abolished. Helping disadvantaged individuals is a worthy cause, but mandating benefits through federal highway funding is inefficient and counterproductive to transportation goals.

Plank 63. Replace the current mass transit grant structure with a single Urban Transit Block Grant.

Federal urban transit assistance has become one of the most wasteful programs in the federal budget. Despite spending about $40 billion of federal funds on urban transit since 1963, ridership is lower today than it was then. The federally-funded transit systems that recently have been built in Detroit, Buffalo, and Miami have been recognized as multi-billion dollar disasters.

To prevent a recurrence of such types of expensive mistakes and to depoliticize the mass transit program, the current grant program should be abolished and replaced with a single Urban Transit Block Grant. Each city's allocation of funds would be based upon objective criteria; such as population density, degree of transit use, and even perhaps an operating efficiency factor, such as operating costs

131

per passenger mile, to reward cities for genuine transit improvements. This new program would allow the cities to establish their own transit priorities, rather than having to follow the arbitrary policies Congress sets for them.

The block grant formula also would alleviate the enormous inequities in the current grant structure. Although all taxpayers support the transit program through the gasoline tax, 70 percent of funds flow to just ten big cities. This apportionment of funds neglects the transit needs of medium and small sized cities.

Plank 64. Create a Space Enterprise Zone.

As with any new commercial endeavor, space business is an extremely high risk activity. To exploit the economic potential of space fully, business must be able to operate within a recognized, administratively flexible environment conducive to its operations. Such a climate would be fostered by a Space Enterprise Zone. This zone would be a designated volume of space between 50 miles and 50,000 miles above the earth, an area referred to as "near earth orbit." In this zone, the government would not compete in any commercial activities that could be performed by private businesses.

This would mean that NASA would not compete for private launches of commercial cargo and that no commercial activities, such as a proposed space station, would be performed in the zone by any NASA vehicle. NASA would confine its activities to basic research, space science, and exploration. The government also would refrain from imposing within the zone federal regulations, such as antitrust laws, that hinder commercial space development. Commercial activities relating to the zone could be made exempt from such laws.

✻   ✻   ✻

STRATEGY

Deregulation, *privatization, and decentralization are needed to reach the goal of safe, efficient transportation at the lowest possible cost to consumers. America's transportation system is too complex to be left under the direction of a few bureaucrats and politicians in Washington. Deregulation and privatization must be pursued to let consumers, through the marketplace, play a greater role in transportation decisions. Similarly, where government involvement is*

necessary, decentralization will bring decision-making out of Washington and closer to the people.

There have been significant successes in transportation over the last decade ranging from deregulation of the airlines, trucking, and railroad industries to the privatization of Conrail. These successes, however, are now under attack and need to be defended vigorously.

OBSTACLES

A major obstacle to innovative transportation reform is the heads of powerful transportation unions. Current federal control of transportation gives labor leaders clear channels for influencing policy. Dispersing control of transportation among the private sector and state and local governments would erode organized labor's influence. Bureaucrats are another obstacle. Privatization obviously would reduce the number of jobs in the federal government, although productive employees likely will retain their jobs in the newly created private enterprises.

A third obstacle is the public's ignorance of transportation issues. This creates an environment hostile to reform. Because of a widespread misunderstanding of the issues, the media too often have taken a dim view of deregulation and privatization. On airline deregulation, for example, they virtually ignore the enormous consumer benefits, attributing problems such as flight delays to deregulation. Worse, much of the public has been led to believe that deregulation has led to unsafe skies; in fact, there have been 30 percent fewer airline accidents since deregulation. A fourth obstacle to reform is the politicians who refuse to give up their pork-barrel transportation projects. Without the projects, officials will have to work harder to please constituents. Pork-barrel politicians oppose deregulation, privatization, and decentralization because these policies erode their power base.

TACTICS

Educate the Public. *Since much of the opposition to transportation reform is the result of a misunderstanding of the issues, the American public needs to be informed of the direct dividends of deregulation, privatization, and decentralization. The benefits consumers now enjoy from airline deregulation, for example, need to be spelled out completely. The myth that deregulation has reduced safety must be exposed.*

Promote Safety. *Air travel in the U.S. is the safest in the world — and the level of safety has continued to increase since deregulation. Similarly, truck and railroad safety has improved since these industries were deregulated. Yet, the issue of safety continues to be used as an argument against privatization and deregulation. Conservatives should*

135

reclaim the issue of safety as their own and argue aggressively for market reforms as a way to increase safety. For instance, they should point out that aviation could be made safer if needed modernization and new investment were made in the airport and air traffic control systems. The bureaucrats and politicians now in charge of the aviation infrastructure have failed to do this. The air traffic control system, for example, could be reorganized as a private firm owned by its users — airlines, private pilots, and even air traffic controllers. This would allow those with a stake in the system to take more responsibility for making it work safely and make the investments necessary to do that.

Take the Offensive. *One reason deregulation is now under attack is the widespread belief that it has caused today's transportation problems. Instead of denying that these problems exist, conservatives must take the offensive and propose market-oriented solutions. Example: under current government control, airports charge a corporate jet only a nominal fee for landing rights, while a fully loaded Boeing 747 may pay thousands of dollars — though each plane may impose the same costs on the system in terms of controller time and airport delay. Conservatives must make the point that airports should apply market principles of supply and demand in pricing their services to reduce air delays.*

Emphasize Federalism. *Transportation needs vary tremendously from city to city, state to state. Common sense* *dictates that states and localities be given the flexibility to make funding decisions based on their own particular needs. Fairness also demands an end to federal control. Federal boondoggles and pork-barrel projects come at the expense of the American taxpayer and benefit powerful interests who lobby Congress. The Urban Mass Transit program, for example, transfers tax dollars from low-income Americans to union-scale transit workers in New York City. And the tax dollars of a farmer in Wisconsin go to subsidize the subway fare of a lawyer in Washington. Conservatives need to offer state and local authority as the fair and rational alternative.*

Offer Privatization as an Alternative to Cutting Services. *Privatization is a way of delivering and improving current government services without burdening the federal budget. Privatization offers an alternative to budget "cuts." Amtrak, for example, is a service on which many communities rely. Rather than terminating the system, conservatives should encourage a private partnership under which employees, management and even riders could own and manage the system profitably.*

COALITION FOR VICTORY

Consumers. *As users of transportation, American consumers pay lower prices and have greater choice in a deregulated transportation industry. Example: airline deregulation has made air travel an affordable option for average*

Americans. Passenger traffic soared after deregulation, from 275 million in 1978 to 418 million in 1986. People who could not afford to fly in 1978 can do so now because of the competition spurred by deregulation. Those who call for airline re-regulation tend to be politicians or businessmen who fly frequently but whose tickets are paid for by the taxpayer or corporate expense accounts. While they may prize most a comfortable seat, lavish meal service, and punctuality, the family travelling to Disneyland or flying to Grandma's and Grandpa's for Christmas is more concerned with affordable tickets.

Consumers also benefit from deregulation in trucking and railroad industries. The new competition in these industries has lowered transportation costs for goods purchased by consumers. For example, partial trucking deregulation has meant tens of billions of dollars in transportation cost reductions, which were ultimately realized by consumers.

Consumer interest groups were very active participants in the 1970s in the battle for deregulation — and were critical to the success of those initiatives. These groups, however, have so far hesitated to push for future reform and sometimes have advocated reregulation. They need to be encouraged to support deregulation policies once again.

Business. *Significant sectors of the U.S. business community benefit from market transportation policies. Air-*

138

*lines, truckers, space-based industries, and highway con-
struction companies obviously gain directly from deregulation and privatization of their industries. Shippers, however,
have benefited the most. As noted above, deregulation has
reduced transportation costs by tens of billions of dollars. As
a result, shippers generally have been enthusiastic supporters
of deregulation.*

Workers and Unions. *Business opportunities mean worker
opportunities. In Britain, the 1982 privatization of the National Freight Corporation, a government-owned trucking
firm, and several other major companies, such as Jaguar
Motors and British Telecom, has given workers an ownership interest in what were once government-owned operations. Privatization of Amtrak, in which employees would
receive shares in the new operation, would give its employees
the economic incentives they lack as government
bureaucrats. Unions that represent such workers should be
encouraged to back privatization efforts. Alternatively,
employee support for privatization can be gained without
support from the established union leadership. In Britain, for
instance, employee-stockholders of privatized firms often
were major backers of privatization, despite the opposition
of their unions.*

Local Government. *Government officials and others who
would want to transfer many responsibilities from the federal
government to the states, counties and cities should embrace*

transportation decentralization, which shifts funding and other major decisions from Washington bureaucrats to state and local levels. Local governments, for example, gain power from decentralization of highway spending.

Chapter Eight

Agriculture

American agriculture is a victim of its own success. Thanks to remarkable advances in productivity on the American farm, the U.S. can feed itself and much of the world with fewer and fewer farmers. This places continuous economic pressure on marginal farmers to leave the land, resulting in social and economic dislocation for many communities. Trying to reverse this trend would be like trying to hold back the ocean tide. Rather than attempting to do this, federal policy should be to ease the long-term transition of marginal farmers leaving the land, while evening out temporary fluctuations in farm income. In addition, Washington should protect the consumer by ensuring that markets operate effectively and by refusing to protect the farmer at the expense of the consumer.

Current agriculture policies however, fail farmers, consumers, and taxpayers. Support prices for commodities drive up food costs and create surplus output. Enormous subsidies are misdirected to large agribusinesses. And tax dollars are wasted in contradictory programs. Example: some farmers are encouraged to overproduce by guaranteed price floors, government purchase of surpluses, and subsidized irrigation programs, while other farmers are paid — under soil conservation programs — to leave their fields idle. In place of these policies, subsidies should be restricted to needy farm families, not distributed widely through across-the-board aid. Mechanisms such as agricultural options markets should be used more extensively to even out farm income without costly subsidies. And contradictory policies which foster greater use of land through irrigation on one hand, and seek to reduce surpluses on the other hand, should be ended.

—— MARKET PRINCIPLES ——

Plank 65. End subsidies to wealthy farmers.

Federal farm programs are usually defended as an essential means of helping struggling farmers, who otherwise would not be able to make it on their own. The truth is, only a small portion of federal farm subsidies ever reaches struggling farm families. These subsidies go disproportionately to wealthy farmers. Example: of the $7.7 billion in direct federal payments in 1985, 13.3 percent went to farms with more than $500,000 in annual sales, who represent only 1.3 percent of all farms. One California company collected over $20 million in agricultural subsidies in 1986. The same year, a Texas company, partly owned by the Crown Prince of Liechtenstein, received $2.2 million in subsidies.

The reason for this maldistribution is that subsidies are calculated not by need, but by the annual production of each farm. This distribution system should be readjusted to reduce farm payments to those who do not need them.

Plank 66. Decouple farm subsidies from production decisions.

Under most current farm programs, payments to farmers are based on the amount they produce. The problem is that this encourages farmers to produce food regardless of market demands. Among other things, this wastes valuable economic resources and creates surpluses which end up in government storage bins. To avoid this, farm payments should be decoupled from production decisions. Farm subsidies should be based on financial need without regard to a farmer's actual production. The production decisions of farmers then would be made only on the basis of the actual marketplace demand for each crop.

Plank 67. Abolish farm marketing orders.

Under certain U.S. farm programs, known as "marketing orders," producers are organized into cartels which can direct the activities of each grower of their particular crop. Some of these marketing orders are relatively harmless, but others — such as those controlling orange and lemon output — limit significantly the type and amount of food sold to the public. Cartels are generally illegal under U.S. law, but cartel decisions under marketing orders are not only legal, but actually enforced by the U.S. government.

The cost to consumers of marketing orders is enormous. They force Americans to pay higher prices for food. Perhaps more important, the program costs the economy tens of millions of dollars in wasteful overproduction. Marketing orders that limit supply should be abolished, either by Congress or administratively by terminating individual marketing orders by the Department of Agriculture.

Plank 68. Encourage agriculture "options" in place of price supports.

The primary objective of federal agricultural price support programs has been to protect farmers against sudden changes in crop prices. Current federal support programs generally allow farmers to borrow money from the government at the beginning of the crop year, pledging the crop as collateral. At harvest time, if the crop price is less than the amount of the loan, the farmer can forfeit his crop and keep the loan money. In effect, the loan creates a price floor for the farmer. It cost U.S. taxpayers $25.8 billion in 1986 alone to make the loans and store the crops.

Agricultural "options" offer a better way to provide price stability for farmers. Under such a system, farmers could buy options from private investors. These options give the farmer the right to sell his crop to the seller of the option at a predetermined price. This would guarantee the farmer a minimum price for his crops. The farmer of course would pay a small fee for the option, which would vary according to market conditions. There would be no cost to the taxpayer.

Agricultural options are already in use to a limited extent for many commodities, including corn, wheat, cotton, and soybeans. Broader use of options, however, is inhibited by federal price support programs which, in effect, provide taxpayer-subsidized options to farmers. Federal price support levels should thus be lowered, to allow greater use of the option alternative.

STRATEGY

T*homas Jefferson wrote that farmers are the most virtuous Americans. Being rooted to the land, they have a spirit and independence not found among other professions. There is an intrinsic pride and dignity in being a farmer. Yet farmers today are being transformed from that self-reliant breed Jefferson wrote of to a welfare-class state of dependency. The goal of farm policy should be to restore the spirit of independence to American agriculture. The debate is over what policies better promote returning dignity and prosperity to the family farm.*

Rather than continuing down the path of governmental control, conservatives seek to restore free enterprise principles to farming. Policies that focus on helping needy fami-

ly farms and building a self-reliant, free market farm economy will revive hope and opportunity in rural America. This can be done through reduced government direction of agriculture. Farmers' decisions on what and how much to plant should be based upon market demand, not on government policy.

The time is ripe for a major reform of agricultural policy. From fiscal 1982 through 1987, the federal government spent over $100 billion to support farmers. This huge six-year cost is greater than the amount spent in the preceding 48 years. The federal government spent $79 billion from the inception of the farm programs in fiscal 1934 through 1981. Yet despite this unprecedented spending, some farmers continued to lose their farms. Clearly, more government involvement is not the answer.

OBSTACLES

Four significant obstacles stand in the way of restoring free market principles to agriculture while recognizing the needs of the family farm. First is the tremendous politicization of the issue. Agriculture is an emotional matter with the family farm rightfully looming large in the nation's heritage. This has been exploited at the expense of the farmer and has helped create the problem from which he now suffers. Invariably, the politicians offer short-term solutions which appeal to sentiment but which create long-term dependency on

147

the federal government for farmers. A second obstacle is those elected officials who see greater government control of production as the solution to current farm woes. Ironically, these advocates call themselves populists, though their policies mean big government control over farmers.

A third obstacle is the federal bureaucracy. Thousands of people are employed by the federal government to administer federal farm programs. Many of these bureaucrats would oppose dramatic new directions in federal agriculture for fear of losing their government jobs. A fourth obstacle to agriculture reform is popular ignorance of farm facts. One of the public's misconceptions is that most farmers are poor and that federal aid goes only to poor farmers.

In addition, certain regional interests may oppose reforms. For example, much of the California and Florida citrus industry would oppose ending marketing orders. And recipients of cheap federal water, located mainly in the West, would balk at paying the cost of water projects.

TACTICS

Most Americans retain a sentimental attachment to the family farm. In fact, polls have shown that even urban Americans strongly support programs to help farmers. Yet few understand how these programs work. Conservatives should stress that helping struggling family farmers requires

148

changing current policies. The key to reforming agriculture is educating the public as well as decision-makers on conservative alternatives to the current system.

Educate Legislators. *With the exception of the members of the congressional agriculture committees, very few congressmen understand farm programs. Conservatives should present members with the facts and offer concrete alternatives that will work better and cost less.*

Educate Taxpayers. *The $100 billion dollars in federal agriculture spending in the last six years did not prevent a farm crisis. Taxpayers thus must be told that money alone cannot solve the farm crisis and that cheaper alternatives exist. Conservatives offer fiscally sound alternatives to current policy.*

Educate Consumers. *American consumers need to know that current policy leads to artificially high prices for such products as citrus fruit, milk, and peanuts. Consumers must be told that the planks in this chapter would lead to lower prices for those and other food products.*

Dispel Myths. *Existing assumptions regarding agricultural policy must be challenged. One myth is that federal subsidies go to farmers in need. The opposite is true. In 1985, for example, nearly one-third of federal payments to farmers went to the 4.1 percent of farms with sales of $250,000 or more;*

149

and more than two-thirds went to farms with annual sales of $100,000 — only 14 percent of all farms.

Publicize Abuses. *Individuals seeking to reduce defense spending successfully drew public attention to their cause by publicizing abuses such as high-priced toilet seats, coffee makers, and hammers. Similar examples of wasteful agriculture spending could be exposed. Example: in 1986, a company partly owned by the Crown Prince of Liechtenstein received $2.2 million in agricultural subsidies.*

Support the Real Family Farm. *Conservatives should emphasize the importance of providing support for small needy farmers while eliminating subsidies to large wealthy ones. This means opposing a subsidy distribution system which pays millions of dollars to large corporate farms. It also means opposing policies that pay farmers based on the amount they produce and supporting policies that pay farmers based on need.*

Offer Concrete Alternatives. *Solutions exist which can help farmers without distorting markets or increasing farmers' dependency. Agriculture options and decoupling, discussed in Planks 66 and 68, are such concrete alternatives. These are free market means of giving family farmers more genuine help than that offered by current policies and liberal proposals.*

Be Populists.   *The enemy of farmers is big government. Traditional big-government policies of Washington led farmers down a road of false promises. Conservative solutions reject big-government policies and seek to restore individual choices and opportunities to farmers.*

COALITION FOR VICTORY

Consumers. *Americans should be informed that higher food costs, due to federal agricultural policies, take money from them just as inflation and tax increases do. To make matters worse, the poor, elderly, and families on fixed budgets are hurt the most because they pay proportionally more of their income for food than do the wealthy. Federal farm policies represent a hidden surtax on their weekly food budget. A market-oriented farm policy would lead to lower food prices for many goods.*

A fair food price coalition should be formed to push for repeal of the surtax on food. The coalition should consist of food manufacturers, food retailers, and consumers — especially the poor, the elderly, and families. The group should identify and publish the hidden costs of federal farm policies to business and consumers. Example: If an average family paid $400 more in 1987 for food due to federal subsidies, a sample rebate check for that amount could be drawn in the name of American families and sent to members of Congress. Other checks could be drawn in the name of the poor

151

and elderly, and restaurants and supermarkets could be encouraged to post "alternate" price lists showing what consumers would pay for non-subsidized food.

Taxpayers. *Annual farm subsidy costs today are several times as large as they were at the beginning of the Reagan Administration. Federal farm programs cost taxpayers $17.7 billion in fiscal 1985, $25.8 billion in 1986, and $22.4 billion in 1987. A more market-oriented agricultural policy would be a boon to taxpayers. Allowing farmers to base their planting decisions on demand rather than government policy would save billions of dollars annually.*

Farmers. *Farmers will be freed from federal dependency by market solutions. Because federal crop supports change annually due to budget pressures, farmers must wait each year for the Secretary of Agriculture to announce the program benefits before deciding what to plant. Most farmers are tired of these often-changing and contradictory programs. Farmers should favor an alternative that liberates them from the constraints of current policy, but would guarantee a living wage during bad crop years. Farmers also will benefit from genuine competition in agricultural markets. Removing government price supports, for example, will make U.S. farm products more competitive, opening up new export markets for farmers.*

Farm Groups. *Farm organizations, such as the American Farm Bureau Federation, should be champions of free market farm policies. Such groups recognize that government controls are no solution to current farm woes and that a return to market-oriented policies is in the farmer's best interests. These groups consistently have advocated market-oriented policies in agriculture and other areas. While they support subsidies, they are interested in making the farmer more independent of the federal government in the long term.*

Food Processing Companies and Retailers. *High prices for farm goods increase costs for food producers and retailers. Pizza Hut, for example, lobbies against dairy price supports which drive up its costs for cheese, while other pizza producers import casein, a cheese substitute, rather than pay the high price for subsidized American cheese. Food producers and retailers employ millions of people whose jobs depend on competitive prices for the goods their employer sells. In the long run, agriculture subsidy policies reduce job creation and job security in these industries.*

153

Chapter Nine

Environment

America's wilderness areas and sensitive animal life is threatened not by big business, but by government bureaucrats and pernicious economic incentives created by government. The reason is that "public ownership" of national parks, forests, and wilderness areas in reality means ownership by nobody. Instead, control is vested in the hands of federal agencies that respond to bureaucratic incentives. Often these are destructive of environmental goals. Anti-pollution policy suffers from a similar disregard of incentives, resulting in policies costly to business and ineffectual in reaching policy goals.

Federal policy should shift to create positive incentives to reach environmental goals effectively and efficiently. To do this the fiction of public ownership should be replaced with the reality of responsible ownership by non-governmental entities. Example: environmental organizations could manage wilderness areas. The private sector,

155

meanwhile, could be required to pay the full cost of gaining access to forest and range lands. The responsibility for hazardous waste programs could be moved to the states and local communities as much as possible, to encourage innovative approaches and to discourage communities from merely passing the buck, and the bill, to Uncle Sam. Finally, privatization and other market-based strategies could introduce strong incentives for efficient pollution policy.

—— Public Lands ——

Plank 69. Create a Wilderness Board to administer wilderness areas.

For decades the management of wilderness areas in the U.S. has provoked bitter political disputes. Wilderness advocacy organizations take every opportunity to get Congress to classify sensitive tracts as wilderness areas. This blocks virtually any commercial use of these tracts. Those who oppose such efforts invariably are denounced as anti-environment. Yet it is possible to balance use and conservation in many sensitive lands. Environmentalists would understand this if they were given the responsibility for

156

running wilderness lands. If they effectively "owned" the land, through a long lease arrangement with the federal government, they would have the incentive to raise revenues from less sensitive lands to purchase more sensitive areas. As with a private museum, the environmental groups could buy and sell tracts for their "collection," and augment their revenues with commercial activities that did not conflict with their primary purpose. In fact, several organizations, such as The Nature Conservancy, already own land privately and obtain revenue by permitting carefully controlled mineral exploration.

A Wilderness Board should be established, consisting of environmental organizations. This Board would manage public lands, making day-to-day decisions over operation of the lands and decisions regarding sales and purchases of lands. The Board would be required to report to Congress, which would have oversight responsibility.

Plank 70. End Forest Service destruction of forests.

The U.S. Forest Service is the nation's largest road builder. The Forest Service road network is more than eight times as long as the federal interstate system and has scarred America's woodlands. Having spent billions of taxpayers' dollars to build these roads, to give access to commercial timber companies, it then sells wood below cost. And in its efforts to give away timber, the Forest Service encourages both the "clear cutting" of forests, which leads to huge gaping holes on thousands of otherwise scenic hillsides, and also the deforestation of sensitive high-elevation timberlands.

The more roads that the Forest Service builds and the more clear-cut areas that must be replanted, the bigger the Forest Service's budget and workforce. Since the Forest Service does not in any sense own forests, the long term damage to the value of forests from its actions, and the artificial economics of timber sales do not concern it.

More productive management of the nation's forests would result from transferring ownership to conservation organizations, or selling essentially commercial forests — with assurances for public access — to commercial timber companies. In both cases, the new owners would have a direct interest in preserving the value of the forests to protect their investment, and in ending uneconomic destruction of trees.

Plank 71. Increase state and local control of hazardous waste policy.

The cleanup of hazardous waste dumps is rapidly becoming the nation's most expensive public works program. Billions of dollars are committed to dealing with the results of toxic emissions. Few Americans would dispute the need to deal with the hazardous waste problem, but it should be done by states and local governments, not the federal government and its Superfund program. Federal responsibility simply allows local officials to escape the obligation to take quick and decisive action before a problem reaches crisis proportions. Meanwhile, paying for cleanup through taxes on all firms, as now is the policy, imposes a double cost on responsible firms which already control their toxic pollution, while allowing the worst polluters to evade the cost of their actions.

Two steps are needed to make hazardous waste policy effective, fair, and economical. First, it must be made clear that it is the responsibility of state and local governments close to the scene to take the initiative in controlling toxic dumping and dealing with its consequences. Second, future hazardous dumps could be limited by instituting a tax on dangerous waste products rather than on all firms in industries producing toxic waste. This would encourage firms to find the least costly way of reducing or safely disposing of waste, and it would place the heaviest tax burden on the worst offenders.

——— Privatization ———

Plank 72. Use market mechanisms, such as a production rights market, to achieve pollution goals.

Virtually all Americans want pollution reduced. And virtually all Americans want to keep their jobs. Yet laws forcing businesses to reduce pollution increase business costs and thus reduce employment. Government policy, moreover, discourages firms from finding the least costly method of reducing pollution. Typically, regulations require a firm to meet a particular emission standard or to install a particular anti-pollution device, irrespective of immediate or long-term cost.

A better anti-pollution policy would mandate industry-wide reductions in pollution, but allow firms more flexibility to meet these standards. The whole industry could reach the standard by encouraging firms that could reduce pollution substantially, but inexpensively, to cut pollution the most. Meanwhile, some other firms, for whom meeting the standard would mean heavy costs and job losses, would be able to exceed the standard. In this way, pollution could be reduced at the lowest possible industry-wide cost. And individual firms would be permitted to find the least costly way of reducing pollution, rather than installing particular equipment.

The way to achieve industry-wide standards while minimizing harm to some firms would be by a "production rights market." The total permissible pollution would be set for an industry, or a group of firms in a particular area, and licenses would be sold for the right to contribute to that total. The revenues collected would be used by government to deal with such effects of pollution as health problems or corrosion of buildings. Polluting firms would have to purchase the licenses but could trade them between each other. The result would be that firms easily able to reduce pollution would do so to avoid licensing costs, while other firms would prefer to pay license fees, rather than facing heavy costs and layoffs. The overall standard would be achieved.

Plank 73. Review Environmental Protection Agency grant incentives to encourage private sector financing and operation of wastewater plants.

The privatization of municipal wastewater treatment plants, which clean and treat sewage, is a recent success story. Cities such as Chandler, Arizona, and Auburn, Alabama, which have contracted with private firms to construct and operate wastewater treatment plants, have reduced costs by about 20 to 30 percent. Because these competitive private firms are more innovative and less costly, the integrity of the water supply is better protected. As such, wastewater treatment privatization has won accolades from environmental groups and local taxpayers.

The current federal grant program, however, discourages privatization. Cities must forfeit their federal funds for wastewater plant construction if they seek private financing. This can make privatization unattractive to cities even when the cost of a privately built wastewater plant is less than the specifications required by an EPA grant. To reverse these perverse incentives the federal government should allow cities to receive 20 percent of a project's cost if it is privately owned and financed. The cost to the federal government would be far less than the 55 percent federal funding that cities currently can receive for publicly owned plants. But because of the significant savings that can be achieved through private design and financing, even with the smaller grant many cities would find it more economic to use the private sector.

*   *   *

STRATEGY

Environmental protection policy and procedures need to be improved. This can be achieved through innovative policies which replace bureaucratic plodding with aggressive free market incentives. While government has a role to play in environmental protection, so does the marketplace. And while pollution control is an important goal, there is a cost in achieving it. This cost is in jobs. Consequently, policymakers should focus on the least costly way of achieving reasonable standards. Such an approach would improve environmental protection, resulting in more cleanup for current expenditures or the same cleanup for less cost.

Environmental reform in the 1990s offers the welcome opportunity of building a partnership between conservatives and traditional liberals. Recently, environmental groups *such as the Audubon Society have recognized the value of partnership with the private sector to achieve conservation goals. And increasingly, such environmentalists are admitting that government is not always the right answer.*

OBSTACLES

One obstacle to innovative environmental solutions is the mindset that the private sector is, by definition, the enemy of a clean environment. This, of course, has served as the rationale for a massive buildup of public sector regulatory industries. Although this mindset has moderated somewhat among certain conservation groups, it remains a significant obstacle to reform. Another obstacle is the federal bureaucracy. A more free market approach to conservation and environmental protection will mean less government spending, and thus fewer bureaucrats.

Congress is another barrier. Federal control over the environment means power for members of Congress. Whether it comes in the form of grass roots support from environmental groups or campaign contributions from industries seeking favors, these benefits are something that politicians do not want to relinquish. And finally, special interests would oppose changes in the status quo. These are of two types: First is the environmentalist on the leftist fringe of the movement who opposes anything that would lessen government control. Second are the lobbyists and industries which benefit from current regulatory policies. Many firms, for example, have learned that environmental policies provide an excellent opportunity to tilt the competitive playing field to favor their interests. Rust Belt industries lobbied hard for "grandfather clauses" in the Clean Air Act which create a bias against new plants in the South and Southeast. Similarly, the restriction on the use of low sulfur coal results from the effective use of environmental laws to benefit the "dirty coal" sector and its union allies. Conservatives should use such examples to explain the environmental risks of relying so heavily on federal environmental regulations.

TACTICS

Make Environmental Protection a Top Priority. *The new political framework for discussing environmental issues must establish that conservatives are committed to a clean, safe environment and preserving America's natural beauty. Liberals and conservatives start from a common, and equally strong, commitment to environmental protection but divide on the question of what means will best achieve that goal. Conservatives must take the offensive and articulate that the environment can be protected by the power of the free market at least cost in money and jobs.*

On December 17, 1969, over 80 members of the House of Representatives jointed in a statement proclaiming the 1970s the decade of the environment. Conservatives should reis-

sue that challenge by proclaiming the 1990s the decade of individual environmental responsiblity. *Just as the 1969 proclamation was followed by a spate of legislative and regulatory initiatives, conservative lawmakers should offer new environmental solutions that call on the responsibilities of individuals and the power of the market to clean and protect the environment.*

Offer a Clean Air Act. *Conservatives in 1988 should take on the challenge of writing a new Clean Air Act that embodies such free market principles as the production rights markets described in Plank 72. Such a competitive Clean Air Act should be the legislative centerpiece of conservative efforts to forge a new coalition of environmentalists.*

Celebrate Earth Day 1988. *Earth Day 1988 should be the launching pad for a new direction in environmental protection. The event should emulate the original Earth Day of April 22, 1970, and promote the idea of completing the job to insure a safe environment for future generations.*

Promote State Level Solutions. *Decentralizing means giving state and local officials more say over environmental policy. State governors should be asked to develop a strategy to: 1) transfer certain environmental programs to states, 2) establish inter-state councils to handle issues of regional concern, and 3) identify environmental issues to be handled by the federal government.*

Work With Rank-and-File Environmentalists. *Most environmentalists are not extremists or socialists. Rank-and-file environmentalists should be given the chance to learn how market-based ideas, rather than big government, are the best way to protect the environment.*

Emphasize the Individual. *True environmentalists accept a direct responsibility for improving environmental quality. Yet, current laws provide almost no direct role for the individual. Current legislation assumes that only companies and products pollute — not people. That failure to enlist the individual has significant cost since much of the ability to improve environmental quality can only be obtained by individual action. Conservatives should develop programs that encourage and allow individuals to play a more active role.*

Encourage Privatization. *Conservatives should enlist private groups with specialized environmental expertise to assume direct stewardship responsibilities for resources now managed by the federal government. Examples would include transfers of Bureau of Land Management caves to speleological organizations or of wetlands to Ducks Unlimited. Conservatives must take the lead in enlisting the energies and enthusiasms of individuals in the environmental effort. Current policy leaves the individual with no task but lobbying Congress for ever more stringent laws and larger* *federal budgets. More creative arrangements would provide a growing number of examples of an alternative approach and make it possible for more and more experiments over time. Chapter IX of the recent Council on Environmental Quality report, "The Private Provision of Public Amenities," provides a number of valuable case studies of past environmental privatization initiatives.*

Publicize Government Environmental Failures. *The problems of current environmental programs must be understood. The current effort to reform federal water policies, to reduce forestry subsidies, and to rethink the sewage grant program was preceded by research projects and articles documenting how these programs were wasting money and endangering the environment. Similar studies are needed for other environmental programs. The public must learn how the Superfund has become a vast public works boondoggle, and how the Clean Air Act encourages the use and continued operation of older, more polluting plants. Also more studies are needed detailing the ways in which environmental regulators discourage the development and introduction of less polluting technologies.*

COALITION FOR VICTORY

Environmental Groups. *Moderate environmentalists and pragmatic conservationists must be part of an environmental coalition. Communication between such groups and con-*

168

servatives must improve. The transfer of public land management from government to conservation groups should become a primary objective. Business now supports a number of forums intended to open a dialogue between the business community and moderate environmentalists. Conservative public interest groups should take part to broaden the topics considered.

Industry. *Industries burdened with bureaucratic red tape and inefficient regulations and those unable to develop resources should welcome private alternatives for protecting the environment which are less costly but more effective. The specific biases against new factories and new processes in the current environmental statutes suggest that businesses in growth areas and in sectors undergoing rapid technological change are natural allies in the fight for rational environmental policies.*

Workers. *Workers benefit from policies which encourage business flexibility to meet environmental standards. Too often, federal government regulations have meant the closing of local plants and loss of jobs. More flexible standards, based on local conditions and market principles will mean better opportunities for industries to meet goals and workers to keep their jobs.*

States and Localities. *Current environmental laws treat all issues nationally. Controls are imposed on cars driven in*

169

remote rural regions because Los Angeles or Denver has a localized pollution problem. Urban New York taxpayers pay subsidies to rural timber developers in Montana. These cross-subsidies should make those communities disadvantaged by specific laws willing to become part of an environmental reform coalition.

Academics. *Research is now underway at universities on the costs and problems associated with current environmental laws. Much of this research is buried in journals and needs to be brought to a wider audience.*

Chapter Ten

Energy

Although energy price decontrol has gone far toward eliminating government obstacles to a free market in energy, other regulations continue to hamper domestic resource development. Falling world oil prices, moreover, are leading to increased U.S. dependence on foreign oil supplies, especially from the unstable countries of the Middle East. In the short term, these cheap oil supplies are good news for American business and consumers; in the long run they could spell enormous economic and political problems if the Arab countries sought to exploit U.S. dependence.

U.S. policy should aim to insure against such a potential disruption. Gasoline taxes or oil import fees, however, are not the solution. Such measures would impose large and immediate costs on the economy, making it less competitive and open the door to permanent protectionism in the U.S. energy industry. Instead, federal policy should aim to increase the potential for obtaining oil from domestic and friendly sources during a supply crisis, as well as to remove the unnecessary barriers to supply today.

Plank 74. Reform land use policy.

The October 1973 Arab oil boycott made Americans painfully aware of the dangers inherent in a heavy dependence on energy from abroad. Today, it is not just energy imports that pose a threat to the nation's economic health and military security, but imports of a whole range of essential energy and mineral resources. This growing natural resource vulnerability is in large part caused by restrictive federal policies that inhibit the development of domestic resource deposits. Preliminary findings of an ongoing study by the Bureau of Mines indicate that mineral leasing is severely restricted on some 342.7 million acres of federal lands in Arizona, Colorado, Oregon, and Washington State. In Alaska, some 59.5 million acres, containing 90 percent of the most promising sources of minerals and energy, are highly restricted.

If America is to avoid a repetition of the economic disruptions of the 1970s, federal policies governing access to the public domain must be reformed in two specific ways. First, no tract of federal land should be closed to mineral or energy exploration and development at least until its

172

potential for mineral and energy resources has been assessed. Second, a review is needed of all tracts of federal land that already have been closed to exploration to determine if they contain resources that can benefit the nation. Once the review is completed, those areas found to contain resource deposits should be opened to exploration and development in an environmentally sound fashion.

Plank 75. Reform resource tax policy.

Since 1969, Congress has enacted a succession of tax changes that impose new costs on energy producers and, at the same time, eliminate many tax benefits that they once enjoyed. These changes inhibit domestic energy production and raise costs to consumers. Typical of the congressional actions have been the elimination of the depletion allowance for oil and gas wells, the imposition of a minimum tax on intangible drilling costs, the imposition of the windfall profits tax, and the imposition of a special Superfund tax on petroleum and petroleum products. The result: energy producers are among the most heavily taxed sectors of the U.S. economy. To make matters worse, these taxes raise the cost of domestic exploration, inhibiting domestic energy development and increasing the need for imports.

A sound energy tax policy requires: 1) repeal of the windfall profits tax; 2) repeal of the Superfund tax on petroleum products; 3) restoration of the depletion allowance for exploratory and development wells; 4) repeal of the so-called minimum tax on intangible drilling costs; and 5) enactment of a tax credit for exploratory and development wells in such frontier areas as Alaska and offshore, where costs and lead times are high.

Consideration should be given to exempting stripper wells from the need to pay royalties to the federal government. Stripper wells are those in the final stages of production. These wells produce only about three barrels per day on average and have extremely high production costs. Although each well's production is modest, in aggregate they represent a large proportion of domestic proved reserves. Many have been abandoned because of high operating costs. Exempting them from royalty payments would extend greatly their useful lives and increase domestic oil production.

Plank 76. Decentralize mine waste regulation.

The Environmental Protection Agency (EPA) regulates hazardous wastes under the provisions of the Resource Conservation and Recovery Act of 1976 (RCRA). Subtitle "D" of RCRA provides for the creation of EPA guidelines for hazardous waste disposal which are then responsibilities of the individual states. Under Subtitle

"C" of the Act, EPA is authorized occasionally to regulate the disposal of hazardous wastes directly. EPA is currently determining whether it will regulate certain categories of mine wastes under Subtitle "C", or instead establish guidelines for state regulation under Subtitle "D."

Between 1970 and 1984, the U.S. mining industry spent $11.1 billion for pollution control equipment. According to an EPA study, the imposition of regulations under Subtitle "C" could result in additional outlays of nearly $10 billion. More important, direct federal regulation could prove impractical. Mine wastes vary enormously in character depending on the local conditions in which they are produced, the types of processing used at each mine, and the specific mineral mined. Federal rules are unlikely to be flexible enough to take such differences into account.

Regulating mine wastes under Subtitle "D", by contrast, would allow state officials familiar with local conditions to determine what specific actions should be taken to dispose of mine wastes safely within a broad set of guidelines established at the federal level. This is the course that EPA should take.

Plank 77. Reduce mineral vulnerability.

The growth of mineral imports from abroad poses a threat to U.S. economic health and military security. Of particular concern is the escalating dependence on communist nations for such strategic minerals essential to the national defense as platinum group metals, chromium, and alloying metals. Commerce Department officials charged with monitoring communist bloc mineral exports to the U.S. have found the increases so large that they are reported in increments of 100 percent.

Two actions can reduce America's growing mineral vulnerability. First, the nation's stockpiles of such strategic minerals as platinum group metals, chromium, and vanadium should be maintained and, in some cases, expanded. Yet efforts are underway to virtually eliminate the stockpiles to generate funds to reduce the federal deficit. This policy generally should be reversed, except for those commodities of which surpluses are stockpiled, such as copper and silver. The surpluses of these latter minerals should be sold. Funds generated from such sales should be applied to the acquisition of other critical commodities whose stockpile levels are inadequate.

Second, the U.S. should develop alternate, secure suppliers of strategic minerals where possible. The best insurance against a disruption of supplies is a diverse group of suppliers. The creation of a diversity of suppliers can be assisted by giving preferred status to those nations geographically close or with governments friendly to the U.S.

STRATEGY

Environmentally sound market-oriented energy policies can assure the nation of the resources to maintain economic health and military security. The market can create incentives for appropriate resource development by assigning resources values commensurate with their worth. Market forces would prevent the squandering and the needless hoarding of commodities. Since markets accurately reflect the values of society as a whole, they will provide for a level of investment in pollution abatement, and other outlays related to the environment, in keeping with the value society assigns such investments.

177

OBSTACLES

Since the late 1960s, some extremist environmental groups and their allies in Congress have placed increasing amounts of public land in highly restrictive categories, effectively blocking mineral and energy resource development in some of the nation's most promising areas. They have accomplished this largely because of a widespread lack of public understanding of the magnitude of this resource lock-up and of its potential consequences. In addition, the groups have mobilized local opposition to attempts to open up specific tracts of land by capitalizing on the "not in my backyard" syndrome. Examples include such areas as the Santa Barbara Channel off the California coast and the Georges Bank off New England.

Obstacles to reducing the tax burden on energy companies include congressional antipathy toward the industry and the misperception that energy and mineral companies are a limitless source of tax funds. Reforming energy taxes at this time runs into opposition from budget cutters.

Obstacles to maintaining an adequate strategic stockpile include the efforts of some Reagan Administration officials who are over-eager to sell all commodities to raise cash to reduce the deficit. Some mineral industry officials, meanwhile, do not want excess commodities sold for fear

178

that this would disrupt commodity markets. This is especially true of silver. As a result, the debate over modernizing the stockpiles has tended to be polarized between two factions, one that would sell nothing, and the other that would sell everything.

TACTICS

Recast the Debate. *Opponents of energy development have been successful in recent years because they have managed to characterize the debate as a moral issue, with advocates of a cleaner environment and better public health and safety pitted against greedy developers who are said to care nothing about the environment or the public. Thanks to this emotive but erroneous portrayal of the issue, supporters of rational energy development have been put on the defensive; the true public interest has suffered. The debate must be recast if pro-development forces are to win a fair hearing. The public's attention must be focused on the consequences of overregulation, including the serious threat to the nation's security and economic health.*

Emphasize the Least Cost Approach. *A critical first step toward a more balanced debate over energy development and use is to emphasize that the issue is not a black-and-white choice between a clean environment or energy development, but a trade-off involving jobs, growth, and environmental protection. The debate should be about how to* *develop and use energy resources at minimum cost to the environment and job opportunities.*

Voice National Security Concerns. *Conservatives must point out that, by blocking energy development, many environmentalists are unwittingly undermining U.S. security by forcing greater dependence on foreign supplies. Reducing this dependency through orderly domestic exploration and development would reduce the need for young American servicemen to risk their lives in the Persian Gulf keeping the sea lanes open for oil tankers.*

Simplify and Personalize the Issues. *The opponents of energy development have used simple language to present their case and have linked their policies to the well-being of average Americans. Thus audiences have been told the issue is Big Oil versus you and me, or big business destroying the national parks. Pro-development forces must counter with simple but accurate messages. They must explain to steelworkers in Pittsburgh, truck drivers in Atlanta, or autoworkers in Detroit that their jobs are on the line if energy costs skyrocket because domestic supplies dry up or foreign supplies are embargoed. They must remind Americans about gas lines. And they must warn mothers and fathers that their sons may have to fight in a Middle East energy war if environmentalists continue to stop efforts to find oil in the Arctic.*

Attack Deliberate Misinformation.   *Environmentalists have specialized in hit-and-run misinformation tactics and inconsistency. Example: in their bid to block exploration and development in Prudhoe Bay, Alaska, radical environmentalists claimed such development would destroy wildlife; this proved to be completely untrue. Instead of dealing with every wild charge levied by the anti-development lobby, supporters of rational energy development should expose its flip-flop positions and seeming disregard for the interests of American workers and consumers.*

COALITION FOR VICTORY

Consumers. *The "oil shocks" of the 1970s burdened the American public with $2 trillion in direct and indirect costs. These included over $500 billion paid for imported energy, substantial increases in unemployment and inflation, and the highest U.S. interest rates since the Civil War. Another oil shock could spell similar disaster. The growing U.S. dependence on foreign oil makes such a situation increasingly likely. Moderate consumer groups should help heighten public awareness of this possibility. Consumers should be taught that a balanced energy and environment policy will yield lower oil and gasoline prices and cheaper manufactured goods.*

Labor. *Fostering domestic energy and mineral exploration would stimulate employment, improve U.S. industry's com-*

181

petitive position, and reduce the threat of another job-destroying oil embargo. Since the enormous costs associated with restrictive federal pollution regulations on business lead to a corresponding loss of employment, labor has a significant stake in an overhaul of regulations.

Industry. *Industry benefits from pro-development energy policies, but it hesitates to get out front on the issue because of the image created by opponents of development. Conservatives should help open a dialogue between industry and moderate environmentalists so that misinformation does not dominate the development debate. Industry should be encouraged to use its resources to educate the public on the costs of overly restrictive development policies.*

State Officials. *The regulation of mine wastes, under RCRA, creates a basic states' rights issue. States traditionally have had responsibility for mine waste regulation. Any attempt to impose broad federal regulations would result inevitably in rules that were either unworkable, or so weak as to be meaningless. State officials should support a strategy of decentralizing the authority for regulating mine wastes.*

Defense Interests. *Key industries dependent on strategic and critical materials include electronics, aerospace, electric power, and communications. Firms in these sectors would work for the maintenance of adequate stocks of the materials essential to their operations. Moreover, major*

182

defense suppliers, veterans' organizations, and other groups sensitive to the threat to U.S. security posed by energy dependence and mineral shortages are likely to back a strong stand on the issue.

Chapter Eleven

Health

Health care costs continue to skyrocket. Since 1981, the cost of medical care has increased at an average near twice the rate of inflation. Between 1965 and 1985, total national expenditure on health care jumped from 5.9 percent of GNP to 10.7 percent of GNP. Spending on federal health care programs has continued to soar as well. From 1975 to 1985, federal spending for Medicare and Medicaid grew from $25 billion to $103 billion per year.

Americans have made it clear that they want universal access, at reasonable cost, to health care services. The only option they have been given so far to accomplish this is the liberal recipe of more taxpayer-financed and government-managed social insurance programs, which already have a long record of cost overrun and poor targeting. Needed instead is a comprehensive approach that combines the goal of universal, dependable coverage and financial protection with a foundation of sound economic principles and realistic political dynamics that allows legislators to back it.

Such a comprehensive approach needs action in three key areas. First, the regulation of health insurance should be reformed to reduce its cost and to require working Americans to obtain adequate protection. Second, the tax treatment of health plans should be amended to encourage companies and workers to shop around for economical and comprehensive coverage and to provide incentives for workers to make more adequate provision for their retirement years. Third, the federal role in health care should be reassessed, with the aim of encouraging states and the private sector to play a greater role in designing and providing services to the poor, the veterans, and the elderly.

— Health Insurance Reform —

Plank 78. Change health insurance regulations and tax treatment to reduce the cost of individual and family policies.

Two of the factors responsible for the high cost of health insurance are the unfavorable tax treatment of insurance company reserve funds and state laws mandating that policies provide specific benefits.

For policies with potentially large liabilities, such as life insurance or catastrophic health insurance, large reserve funds are necessary. Every dollar taken in taxes from reserve funds is a dollar that cannot be used to expand the reserves through investment or to pay claims. One of the factors making life insurance affordable for most Americans is that the reserve funds for these policies are not taxed. Health insurance reserve funds are taxed at the standard corporate rate. Reducing or eliminating the taxes on reserve funds for health insurance, particularly for catastrophic acute and long-term care policies, could help make those policies more affordable.

187

There are now over 600 separate state laws requiring health insurance policies to include coverage for specific medical services or providers. When states mandate that health insurance policies pay for specific providers or procedures (examples: optometrists, chiropractors, mental health treatments, and physical therapy), they essentially establish monopolies in medical care. Mandated benefits guarantee markets for the favored providers and force insurance companies to pay whatever those providers charge. This has had the predictable result of encouraging: 1) an increase in the number of providers offering the favored service, 2) an increase in the use of the service by policy holders, and 3) an increase in the fees charged by the providers. All this drives up health care costs unnecessarily. The federal government should look for ways to encourage the states to repeal their mandated benefit laws and should avoid introducing any new federal laws mandating benefits.

Plank 79. Require individuals to purchase catastrophic health insurance or pre-paid health plans for themselves and their families.

Most Americans believe that access to health care should be available to all of their fellow citizens. The problem is that, while well-off Americans usually can afford to pay most of their medical expenses and while the poor and other groups are protected through federal programs, many others who can afford protection prefer to play Russian roulette with their own and their families' health. When costly illness strikes such a family, either they are ruined financially, go without treatment, or have their care costs covered by more prudent citizens who feel obliged to do so.

Liberals tend to argue that the plight of these uninsured or underinsured Americans must be addressed through a taxpayer-financed health system for virtually all Americans or by forcing corporations to pay for comprehensive health benefits. But this would lead to a very expensive system of doubtful quality to serve a minority of Americans or to a significant increase in business costs and concomitant job losses.

A better approach is to recognize that Americans who can afford insurance, but decline to procure it, should not be free riders on the rest of society. Instead, they should be required by law to purchase protection, at least for their dependents and preferably also for themselves, so that society is not held hostage to its own sense of compassion. This would be similar to current policies requiring auto owners to have liability insurance.

Plank 80. Reform medigap insurance rules to cover all non-Medicare reimbursed charges over $2,000 instead of current "first dollar" coverage.

Despite all the federal spending for Medicare, the program still leaves the elderly unprotected against high catastrophic expenses for care by doctors and hospitals. Most of the elderly gain supplemental protection against such costs through private medigap insurance. But federal regulations make this insurance unnecessarily costly by requiring that it cover lesser up-front costs as well as more expensive catastrophic burdens.

These regulations should be changed to require more coverage of high catastrophic costs and to reduce the required coverage for more routine up-front costs. More specifically, the law should require private insurance to cover all doctor and hospital charges not reimbursed by Medicare over $2,000 per year. Companies would be able to offer insurance covering more of the first $2,000 on an optional basis.

This change would provide more essential catastrophic coverage for the elderly at reduced cost, since it is the coverage for the up-front, more routine medical charges that makes the insurance so expensive. The lower costs for basic coverage could allow even more of the elderly to obtain private insurance protection against catastrophic medical expenses.

—— Taxation ——

Plank 81. Shift most health care tax breaks from the corporate to the individual tax code to encourage individuals to purchase insurance and medical services directly.

About 80 percent of all health insurance policies are purchased by employers as group policies for their workers and their dependents. This makes health insurance premiums prohibitively expensive for individuals or families to purchase on their own. And the third party payment system which this creates removes all the normal consumer incentives to question costs, since the consumer (patient) pays little of the bill either directly or indirectly (through insurance premiums) with the result that health care costs continue to escalate rapidly.

It is necessary to create an incentive structure that encourages consumers to question the need and cost of all the health care they purchase but does not prevent them from obtaining needed care because of its expense. The most effective and equitable way to do this is to use the personal tax code to shield Americans from heavy medical costs while encouraging them to make economical choices. Consumers should be encouraged to replace employers as the direct purchasers of insurance for expensive and unpredictable medical needs and to pay out of their own pockets for more predictable less expensive health care items.

This can be accomplished by transferring most health-related tax breaks from the corporate to the individual tax code. Currently, individuals and families can deduct only those medical expenses that exceed 7.5 percent of adjusted gross income. Instead of this there should be separate tax deductions for expenditures on health insurance premiums, coinsurance payments, and unreimbursed medical expenses. Taxpayers should be allowed to deduct a large percentage of their unreimbursed medical expenses, a lesser percentage of their coinsurance payments, and a small percentage of their health insurance premiums. In addition, taxpayers should be allowed to take these deductions above the line, that is, without itemizing other deductions and in addition to the standard deduction.

Plank 82. Make corporate plans for retiree health insurance tax deductible.

Millions of retired Americans today enjoy private health insurance coverage supplementing Medicare, paid for by their former employer as part of their pension benefits. A valuable addition to such coverage would be employer-sponsored programs that build savings during working years to pay for nursing home care insurance in retirement. This would be a major step toward financing long-term care for the elderly.

Recent changes in the federal tax code, however, discourage employers from providing such benefits. Employees are no longer allowed to deduct their contributions to reserve funds used to finance health benefits for their retirees. As a result employers have reduced health benefits for their retirees when they should be expanding them.

This tax policy should be reversed.

193

Plank 83. Exempt health care tax deductions for needy relatives from the current dependent support test.

Under current law, a taxpayer who wishes to deduct any expenditures on behalf of a dependent must demonstrate that he or she provided at least 50 percent of the dependent's total support for the year. This dependent support test hinders taxpayers from helping relatives who are financially independent for the most part but in need of some assistance. Such individuals are likely to be elderly relatives living on fixed incomes or adult children who have just left home but work at low paying jobs. They are also the individuals most likely to have inadequate health insurance.

In calculating their deductible medical expenses, taxpayers should be allowed to include any payments made for medical care or insurance on behalf of a relative included as a dependent on the taxpayer's health insurance, regardless of whether that relative qualifies as a dependent for other tax purposes. This would encourage families to assume more of the health care costs for medically or financially needy relatives. It would make families the second line of defense against medical costs — behind insurance but ahead of government.

Plank 84. Support Health Care Savings Accounts.

The current Medicare system is a shambles. The program faces dramatic long-term financing problems, requiring payroll tax increases of 100 percent to 400 percent or benefit cuts of equivalent magnitude. Yet today's very high payroll taxes already reduce employment and economic growth. At the same time, Medicare's benefit structure has broad gaps that leave the elderly unprotected from high medical expenses including the costs of nursing home care.

Bipartisan legislation already introduced in Congress would begin countering these problems by establishing Health Care Savings Accounts (HCSAs). Workers and their employers could contribute to these accounts during working years in return for income tax credits. In retirement, workers would use these accounts to purchase insurance to cover more routine medical expenses, or to pay such expenses directly, rather than relying on Medicare. Medicare would cover catastrophic expenses for care by doctors and hospitals. Funds in the account also would be available to purchase insurance against the high costs of nursing home care.

195

This private option could eliminate the long-term financing crisis of Medicare by reducing reliance on the program, increasing reliance on private savings and insurance, and avoiding the need for future dramatic payroll tax increases. At the same time, the combined HCSA/Medicare system would eliminate the current critical gaps in Medicare coverage. New incentives would be created to counter rapidly rising health costs, as workers seeking to preserve their HCSA funds would be more cost-conscious. This option could complement the new voucher system proposed under Plank 85 with workers substituting the accounts for some or all of their vouchers.

— Reforming the Federal Role —

Plank 85. Convert Medicare, Medicaid, and veteran's health care programs to voucher systems.

Runaway health care costs can be countered by converting Medicare, Medicaid, and veteran's health benefits into voucher systems. Each beneficiary of these programs would receive a voucher equal to the average expenditure per beneficiary in each program. The vouchers could purchase medical care through a private insurance company or a health maintenance organization (HMO). As long as beneficiaries purchased at least minimum coverage against catastrophic illness, they could be allowed to convert unused vouchers into cash at the end of the year.

Such a system would make consumers and providers far more cost-conscious, imposing incentives to economize throughout the medical care system. Consumers would be more concerned about avoiding unnecessary services or unnecessarily costly care. Doctors, hospitals, insurers, HMOs, and health product manufacturers would recognize the increased consumer sensitivity to cost and compete to devise new ways to keep costs down.

The vouchers also would give beneficiaries more freedom of choice concerning their health care. This would be particularly important for the poor, who could avoid Medicare mills where services and care are generally substandard. With the vouchers, the poor could participate in mainstream medical care system.

Plank 86. Contract for private sector veteran's care.

The federal government provides health benefits to veterans and their families through government-built and run Veteran's Administration (VA) hospitals. These facilities are very costly to build and operate, are highly bureaucratic and offer questionable quality of care. The entire VA hospital system costs the federal government over $10 billion per year. Since many older veterans move to different cities or retirement communities when they retire, the veterans' hospitals in northern industrial cities have fewer patients and higher maintenance costs for older buildings. Those in states such as Florida are inadequate to meet the new demands.

To reduce the costs and improve the quality of veterans' care, the federal government should contract with private hospitals and health maintenance organizations to provide health benefits. Contracts for veterans in each area could be granted under a competitive bidding process, with several facilities awarded the responsibility of serving veterans in each locality. Current government-owned VA hospitals could then be sold to private owners and operators.

As a result of these changes, the cost to the federal government of providing these benefits would be reduced sharply. Veterans could obtain health care in the same quality mainstream system that serves most Americans.

Plank 87. Contract with corporations to provide Medicare services for their retirees.

Major American corporations have become leaders in designing health care plans. Faced with rapidly escalating health insurance costs, they are experimenting with innovative ways to keep workers healthy while keeping costs down. When these workers reach retirement, however, they move to the Medicare system, which generally has not kept up with the innovation in the private sector. Sometimes Medicare will not even pay for cost-saving services that were available at the workplace.

The federal government should negotiate with major firms to provide Medicare services for their retirees. Many of these firms can organize health care services less expensively than most Medicare-reimbursed institutions.

STRATEGY

Conservatives seek to create a comprehensive health care system that serves every American who needs care. The current scheme of federally subsidized and heavily regulated health care is too rigid. This results in poor service, spiraling costs, and bureaucratic inefficiencies that waste taxpayers' money. A more flexible, market-oriented system of comprehensive health care could give Americans more choice: a system where competition encourages quality care at reasonable cost.

Recent efforts to control health care costs have made the system increasingly unsatisfactory even for groups that in past years found it profitable. Health care providers no longer receive open-ended subsidies from programs such as Medicare and Medicaid, but instead face ever tighter price controls and growing paperwork. Beneficiaries are beginning to question just how much they benefit from a system that lowers the quality of care while ignoring some of their most important needs, such as long-term care for the elderly. And corporations are finding that even their tax breaks for employee health insurance no longer compensate for the enormous expense and the problems associated with funding and managing those programs.

OBSTACLES

Given the growing consensus that the current U.S. health care system is flawed, it might be expected that there would be little opposition to major reform, except from the bureaucrats whose jobs are managing the current system. Yet two significant, though intangible, obstacles exist to health care reform. The first is the common tendency of individuals to fear that they could find themselves worse off under a new system. This is especially true with such a personal issue as health care, where suggestions for change invariably raise fears of reduced benefits. The second major obstacle is the way that policy makers, and the public in general, currently think about America's health care. They seem to assume that the health care market, uniquely, is not subject to the normal economic laws of competition governing goods and services. And they seem to assume that only employers or the government can fund health insurance adequately.

Because these and other attendant assumptions have not been challenged seriously in several decades, they have the power of conventional wisdom. The result is that almost all new proposals in health care financing start off on the wrong foot by taking the existing system as a given and then attempt-

ing to graft modifications onto it. Not surprisingly, the benefits of new health care legislation and policies are proving to be increasing limited and unsatisfactory.

TACTICS

Challenge Existing Assumptions. *The existing assumptions about health care financing should be challenged, particularly the belief that health care is not subject to the normal economic laws of competition and that only the government or employers can fund health insurance adequately. In place of this, a new framework should stress individual choice and market competition as innovative reforms that will provide better health care for Americans. The new framework should approach health policy from the perspective of the needs of consumers or patients. In "selling" health care reform, supporters will need to demonstrate not only how the nation as a whole will gain, but also how such specific groups as consumers, workers, and the elderly will benefit.*

Emphasize Omnibus Reform. *Sweeping omnibus health care reform legislation should be drafted based on the new framework and policies. This can be done either by the administration or by a coalition of congressmen. This omnibus health care reform legislation should launch a national debate on health care. The rationale and benefits of reform*

202

should be explained, while the anticipated fears and reservations about the reforms should be allayed.

Explain the Benefits of Choice. *A successful campaign to reform health care policy must point out the tangible benefits to users. Plank 85, for example, proposes vouchers for Medicare, Medicaid, and veterans health care programs. Plank 86 proposes contracting with the private sector for veteran's health care. Supporters of these reforms need to communicate to current recipients how the new system will benefit them. Example: a document should be produced that shows what vouchers and contracting out would give them compared to what they receive under the current system. Veterans and others need to be convinced that conservative reforms not only offer choice, but better services than currently exist.*

Propose Individual Tax Cuts. *Plank 81 proposes shifting health care tax breaks from corporations to individuals, and Plank 83 liberalizes deductions for individuals who care for sick and needy relatives. These proposals should be introduced as legislation this year. The legislation should serve as a base for building political momentum for omnibus health care reform.*

COALITION FOR VICTORY

Consumers. *Shifting health care tax breaks from corporate to personal taxpayers would give individuals and families greater responsibility for their own health care. Most consumers should welcome this responsibility because it carries with it the added security of direct control over a vitally important, but often worrisome, aspect of their lives. A consumer-oriented approach to health care also would encourage cost and quality control. Consumer choice is the most powerful way to encourage providers to offer quality products or services at reasonable costs. Patients and their relatives always have the greatest interest in the quality of care. Strengthening the incentives for them to question the cost and quality of care will bring some measure of control back to a system that sorely needs it.*

Workers. *While some workers, particularly the highest paid, might lose the tax advantages of employer-paid health care, all workers would receive more favorable treatment for their medical expenses on their personal income tax and better protection from large medical bills. For workers in businesses providing little or no health coverage, this change could be a major improvement. It also would be a practical response to current trends in the nation's workforce, such as greater mobility and job changes, two earner couples, and single parent families, all of which have made tying health* *benefits to employment increasingly burdensome. Workers would be able to carry their insurance with them when they changed jobs.*

Unions. *Unions should have few objections to this reform. In the past, unions have sought increased benefits as an alternative to higher wages. Removing health benefits from the equation would put unions in a strong position to demand compensatory increases in cash wages.*

Business. *While businesses would lose most of their current health care tax breaks, they would benefit by being freed from the considerable cost of providing and administering large-scale employee health plans. Even if businesses compensated for this by increasing salaries across the board, they would be able to reduce the accounting and paperwork expense of processing payrolls and managing benefit plans.*

The Poor and Elderly. *Converting Medicare and Medicaid would help current beneficiaries of these programs. While the more affluent elderly would have to pay a greater share of their own medical costs, the elderly as a whole would receive much better protection against catastrophic medical costs. In particular, the combination of vouchers, lower taxes on insurance company reserve funds, and the exemption of medical expenses from the dependent support test, could make long-term care insurance effective and affordable. The elderly also would be relieved of the uncertainty* *and confusion generated by the present, overly complex Medicare system. For both the poor and the elderly, vouchers would provide greater choice in obtaining medical care and would reverse many of the current incentives for providers to lower their costs by lowering the quality of care.*

Insurance Companies. *Although recalculating policies to accommodate the shift from employer group policies to individual and family policies would make extra work for insurance companies, health care reform would benefit insurers in several ways. First, converting current government health programs to vouchers would expand greatly the health insurance market. Second, regulatory relief would be provided by eliminating state-mandated benefits. Third, insurers would have considerable flexibility in writing policies and increased incentives for competition and innovation.*

Health Care Providers. *Health care reform would stimulate greater competition among health care providers, while allowing them much greater flexibility in responding to innovations in medical technology. Some providers may view increased competition unfavorably. But they would benefit by being freed from the massive regulatory oversight and paperwork burdens now imposed by Medicare, Medicaid, and private insurance companies.*

Chapter Twelve

Housing and Urban Development

Federal housing policy should ensure that Americans are adequately housed. To achieve this, the government need neither be a landlord nor in the construction business. Instead of building public housing or contracting with private developers to build special housing for the poor, as it now does, the federal government should give housing vouchers to the poor. To improve the condition of existing public housing projects, tenant management and ownership should be encouraged. And to restrict federal subsidies only to those who need help, the government should privatize federal mortgage agencies.

Firm action is needed to end the fraudulent practice by some mayors and activists of exploiting homeless Americans to extort federal aid, while avoiding solutions to the homeless problem. As such, federal law should be amended to deny housing assistance to communities that reduce the supply of housing through rent control, and to states and cities that continue to discharge mentally ill Americans onto the streets without assuring adequate community care facilities.

Economic development of localities is not a proper federal domain. It is the role of states and communities which have a more direct interest in the costs and benefits associated with government projects aimed at stimulating local economic growth. For this reason, all responsibilities for local economic development should be returned to the states. The only proper role for the federal government is encouraging innovation at the state level through tax and regulatory relief.

— REDEFINING THE FEDERAL — ROLE

Plank 88. Abolish local economic development programs.

The federal government in 1986 provided several billion dollars in subsidies to corporate and business enterprises through a variety of so-called economic development programs — Urban Development Action Grants (UDAG), the Economic Development Administration (EDA), the Small Business Administration (SBA) and others. The record reveals, however, that these programs do not stimulate increased economic activity but merely shift economic investment and activity away from the most efficient and needed enterprises as indicated by consumers in the marketplace, toward projects with politically influential backers. These federal programs are used as political "slush funds" by elected officials to reward their most powerful supporters. Such programs are true "trickle down" economics, with federal funds intended for the poor being siphoned off by wealthy developers and business operators who use them to finance projects from which the poor are supposed to benefit.

The programs provide few concrete benefits to the disadvantaged and needy. They have been used heavily, for example, to subsidize hotel construction by major national chains and for the building of luxury housing and office buildings, with few, if any, net new jobs for the poor and disadvantaged. One of the largest UDAG grants ever went to the $600 million Copley Place luxury development in Boston, which includes a $150-$200 per day Westin Hotel and an upscale shopping mall.

These federally funded economic development programs should be abolished. If business projects are worthy, businesses can raise the funds they need in the marketplace. The only effective way to stimulate economic development and growth is by adopting general free market policies of low taxes, deregulation, privatization, reduced government spending and borrowing, and sound monetary policies to keep inflation down.

Plank 89. Abolish the Department of Housing and Urban Development.

The U.S. Department of Housing and Urban Development has three basic functions: 1) administering programs to provide housing assistance to low income Americans; 2) stimulating the wider availability of mortgages by providing mortgage insurance through the Federal Housing Administration (FHA) and by buying and selling outstanding mortgages through the Government National Mortgages Association (GNMA) and Federal National Mortgages Association (FNMA), thereby creating a secondary mortgages market; and 3) administering such economic development programs as the Urban Development Action Grant Program (UDAG), and the Community Development Block Grant Program (CDBG).

HUD low income housing assistance efforts should be consolidated into a housing voucher program to be administered by the Department of Health and Human Services in conjunction with the other low income assistance programs. FHA should be privatized, as most mortgage insurance today is already provided by private insurers. GNMA and FNMA too should be privatized, as private sector firms have shown that they can maintain a secondary mortgage market. HUD's economic development programs should be discontinued, for they add nothing to real economic growth. Rather, they shift resources away from the marketplace and provide subsidies to enterprises with politically influential and powerful backers.

Should these policies be adopted, no essential functions for HUD would remain. All of HUD's programs could be administered by other agencies, privatized, or abolished. Consequently, HUD itself could and should be abolished.

—— RESTORE MARKET —— FORCES IN HOUSING

Plank 90. Replace low income housing assistance with vouchers.

There are a number of problems with federal housing programs. For one thing, they construct new housing for about twice what it would cost the private sector. For another, the poor have no say in determining the type of housing built for them and end up crammed into what invariably become run-down, neglected, unsafe housing projects which seem to stigmatize them and undermine their efforts to escape from poverty. Most of the poor, moreover, never even manage to get an apartment under these federal programs, because construction is so slow and costly.

Federal housing construction programs are too flawed to be reformed. They must be replaced by housing vouchers. Each low income beneficiary would receive a voucher each month worth a certain amount of money. This would turn the poor into consumers as they used the voucher to pay for rental housing of their choice.

The vouchers would create new demand for housing by the poor. This new demand would stimulate the private construction and rehabilitation of low income housing. If experience is a guide, this would cost much less than government construction. The vouchers also would allow the poor to choose from available housing within each community. Segregating poor Americans into unsafe and badly maintained public projects could be avoided. The poor could participate in the same general private housing market as everyone else. Many more of the poor could receive federal housing assistance through the vouchers, at less total cost to the taxpayer.

Plank 91.   Privatize the Federal Housing and Mortgage Agencies.

The Federal Housing Administration (FHA) was created in 1933 to insure home mortgages to increase their availability. But today private firms insure most mortgages. Similarly, the Government National Mortgage Association (GNMA), the Federal National Mortgage Association (FNMA), and the Federal Home Loan

Mortgage Corporation (FHLMC) were created in subsequent years to buy and sell mortgages to create a secondary mortgage market that would make mortgages more attractive for lenders. But today a healthy private secondary market has been developed.

These agencies should be privatized completely, eliminating unnecessary government interference in the private mortgage market. These agencies are co-opting functions which can be performed at least as well in the private sector. Over the long run, the flexible, competitive private sector will serve consumers better than government can.

FNMA and FHLMC already have been privatized in large measure. The job should be completed by eliminating remaining government ties and subsidies to these corporations. GNMA should be phased out by allowing FNMA and FHLMC to take over its operations for FHA insured mortgages. FHA should restrict its insurance to lower income homebuyers, leaving the market to cover the rest, and test whether private insurance is feasible even for the lowest income buyers.

214

—— THE HOMELESS ——

Plank 92. Offer federal housing aid only to cities that do not control rents.

A number of cities control housing rentals. These controls discourage developers from building rental housing and owners from maintaining existing rental housing. Predictably, this sharply reduces the rental housing supply. Also predictably, tenants tend to hold on tenaciously to existing housing with controlled low rents and keep larger apartments than they often need. This too reduces available rental housing. The result is a severe rental housing shortage, a situation confirmed repeatedly by economic studies and analyses.

With new building stymied and current tenants refusing to budge from their low-rent housing, rents on apartments that do become vacant understandably tend to skyrocket. Tenants often will sublet units at exorbitant rates. As a result, new tenants, ultimately meaning most tenants, face much higher rents than would prevail if rent controls had never been adopted. The damage of such housing policies can be seen most clearly in New York City, which has had rent control since World War II. The city contains vast stretches of badly deteriorated and ultimately abandoned rental housing and suffers from a severe rental housing shortage, sharply limited supplies of new rental housing, and astronomical rents.

The federal government spends billions of dollars each year on programs to increase the available supply of housing. These funds in effect are wasted when given to cities that impose rent control. Federal taxpayers should not pay for new housing for cities that destroy their own housing with rent control. Federal housing funds consequently should be given only to cities that have no rent control.

Plank 93. Amend the 1963 Community Mental Health Centers Act to stop mentally ill Americans from being turned onto the streets.

The most tragic cases of homelessness in America are the mentally ill, wandering aimlessly and lacking medical attention. They constitute the majority of the homeless in some cities and are the innocent victims of local power politics. Under the 1963 Community Mental Health Centers Act, state and city mental hospitals are permitted to release certain categories of chronically ill patients if community based facilities are available for them. Some states are using this as an opportunity to discharge

216

thousands of costly patients even though there are no facilities for them in the community. These patients too often roam city streets. Worse still, these desperately ill Americans are now being used by the same states and cities who threw them out of institutions as pawns in the "homelessness" game to secure more development funds from the federal government — ostensibly to house the homeless.

The federal government should denounce this strategy for the cruel ploy that it is. In addition, the 1963 Community Mental Health Centers Act should be amended to penalize any state that discharges patients without providing adequate alternative care. Until cities and states face such penalties, Americans in need of expert care will continue to be homeless, sitting on sidewalks and laying on park benches.

✳ ✳ ✳

STRATEGY

A*ll citizens in a society as civilized and affluent as the United States should have access to decent and affordable shelter. But this does not mean that the federal government*

should be in the business of constructing housing; it means only that government has an obligation to help those without the means to obtain shelter. Cities and states are the proper levels of government to foster local or regional economic development. The purpose of the federal government is not to subsidize individual firms or to support local urban development projects, but to establish an attractive national climate for enterprise. Consequently, most of the functions of the federal Department of Housing and Urban Development could be eliminated or transferred to other agencies.

OBSTACLES

A broad coalition of interest groups resists reform of housing and development programs. Among the strongest is the construction industry and its unions, which vehemently oppose any reduction in federal construction, with its artificially high wage rates. Another key obstacle is cities and states, which see HUD as a vehicle for obtaining federal dollars. Most big-city mayors for this reason have jumped onto the "homelessness" bandwagon, trying to blame Washington for their own mistakes and using the homeless as pawns to win more federal money. In addition, the quasi-independent mortgage agencies have proven formidable lobbyists for keeping control of part of the mortgage market.

TACTICS

Denounce Exploiters of the Poor. *Conservatives should attack those who mouth concern for the poor, yet pocket most of the funds intended to help the poor. The welfare hotel operators, construction companies, public housing agencies, and others who prosper from federal programs need to be exposed and put on the political defensive, as they were in the recent successful campaign for federal legislation to permit tenant management and purchase of public housing. Similarly, certain mayors should be attacked for exploiting the homeless as an excuse to leverage federal funds for policies that reduce the availability of housing.*

Push for Housing Vouchers. *Conservatives need to press hard for wider use of housing vouchers as an alternative to expensive public housing and federally sponsored private housing for the poor. Not only would vouchers be a less expensive means of housing the poor, enabling more families to be housed, but vouchers would give the poor the right to choose where they want to live, rather than have government bureaucrats segregating them into ghettos. Administrative actions should be taken to force housing officials to make wider use of vouchers already authorized under current law. Meanwhile, low income neighborhood organizations, many of which support vouchers, should be encouraged to pressure Congress for a larger voucher program.*

219

Show How Programs Destroy Housing. *Many urban programs continue because most Americans believe that they help lower-income families. Conservatives need to point out how government-funded projects often have precisely the opposite effect. Example: many Urban Development Action Grants fund the demolition of low income housing and single room occupancy hotels — which traditionally have housed older men — to make way for convention centers and new shopping malls for the middle class. This has added to the problem of shortages of affordable low income housing and exacerbated homelessness. Example: rent control has not helped the poor. It has discouraged landlords from renting out controlled properties. The result: buildings are converted for sale to middle-class buyers, and young professionals with good connections obtain rent-controlled apartments in the central cities.*

COALITION FOR VICTORY

Self-Help Groups. *Many neighborhood organizations now recognize that housing and urban policies do little for the poor and much for developers, unionized construction workers and the middle class. These self-help groups have shown that they are willing to consider conservative proposals to help the poor and are willing to join forces with conservatives to win political victories for the poor. This is how the Housing and Community Development Act was* *passed in 1987. Many smaller homeless shelter operators share conservative anger at the exploitation of the homeless by publicity-seeking politicians. Powerful allies thus exist for those prepared to argue the case for rent decontrol, reform of mental illness policies, vouchers, and other tools to help the poor.*

The Middle Class. *Guilt can be a very effective stimulus to political action. Liberals long have exploited this. Conservatives can turn the tables by focusing on examples of affluent families living in rent controlled apartments while government-subsidized homeless poor roam the street outside. They should highlight the luxury hotels and boutiques that stand where once there were homes for low income Americans. They should challenge middle-class organizations to back proposals which would correct past mistakes. The American middle class could be won over to support policies that actually will help their poorer fellow citizens.*

Financial Institutions. *Wall Street financial institutions rallied around proposals to sell federal loan assets to the private sector in 1987, just as they supported the plan that year to sell Conrail, the federally owned freight railroad. These institutions recognize the commercial opportunities created by such public policy decisions. They prove to be effective and persistent lobbyists and were key to the success of those legislative campaigns. The full privatization of the federal mortgage institutions offers similar opportunities for*

221

the private sector, since private firms would take over the business and no longer would face competition from Uncle Sam. Thus private financial institutions could be strong backers of plans to privatize the housing and mortgage agencies. Home builders and realtors too should be brought into the coalition to privatize federal mortgage institutions. They have a significant interest in reforms that would enhance competition in mortgage markets.

Religious Organizations. *Church leaders should be encouraged to support approaches that foster individual responsibility and pride of ownership among the poor. Conservatives should work with religious organizations to strengthen private initiatives to aid the poor. Many black churches in Washington, D.C., are active in providing low-income housing through cooperative privatization efforts. Example: members of the Church of the Savior, including developer James Rouse, formed the Enterprise Foundation to provide low-income housing. The foundation's first full-scale venture, Jubilee Housing Project, led to the renovation of more than two hundred apartments.*

Chapter Thirteen

Welfare

America's welfare system suffers from three serious flaws. It is too centralized, which leads to misallocation of resources and the bureaucratic suffocation of local initiative. It is based on the doctrine of welfare rights, which means that the poor are not encouraged to improve their condition in return for assistance. And it is dominated by a middle-class "poverty industry" of service providers, who discourage self-help and effectively force the poor to accept their services at taxpayer expense. The result is that instead of a compassionate system that works against poverty, America has a costly, bureaucratic system that entrenches dependency.

If America is to win its War on Poverty, the welfare system must be reformed. First, greater discretion must be given to states, the proved innovators of welfare policy to pursue new welfare strategies. Second, incentives must be given to states to end welfare dependency. Third, the idea

223

of mutual obligation must be reintroduced into welfare policy through such means as workfare requirements and tough action to enforce child support. Fourth, vouchers and other "empowerment" mechanisms should be introduced to break up the poverty industry that currently inhibits self-help efforts. And fifth, tax and benefit structure disincentives to self-reliance should eliminated.

—— DECENTRALIZE ——

Plank 94. Decentralize decision making to states and localities and give federal grants only to poorer states.

States are the cutting edge of welfare policy. The states are experimenting with workfare, new ways to end dependency, and proposals to improve Medicaid. Congress is merely playing catchup. The trouble is that the states' ability to explore new ideas in welfare or to tailor programs to local circumstances is restricted by the federal grant and regulatory process.

Two steps are needed to achieve decentralization while protecting the interests of the poor. First, states should be

permitted to ask for waivers from existing program rules
to enable them to combine or reorganize existing welfare
programs, and thereby, to mount a more effective attack
on poverty and dependency. States can already do this in
the case of Medicaid. They should be allowed to do so with
all welfare programs. Second, the federal grants programs
should be overhauled. Currently many rich states receive
generous federal assistance, while many poor states get insufficient help. The grant structure should target federal
dollars only to states that cannot meet their welfare obligations with state funds (see Plank 6).

Plank 95. Cut federal contributions to states with high welfare benefits.

In many states the combined welfare benefits received
by many families through programs such as Aid to
Families with Dependent Children (AFDC), food stamps,
Medicaid, and public housing greatly exceed income
designated as poverty level. For example, in California
the average family of three on welfare will receive $10,125
per annum from the AFDC, food stamp, and Medicaid
programs. The poverty level for a family of three is currently $8,738. High welfare benefits obviously discourage
work, promote dependency, and weaken families by undermining the role of the breadwinner.

The federal contribution to welfare spending in states with high welfare benefits for able-bodied adults should be limited so that in no case will the combined benefits of food stamps, AFDC, and Medicaid be able to exceed poverty-level income.

— RESTORE INDIVIDUAL — RESPONSIBILITY

Plank 96. Enact authentic workfare legislation.

One child in ten in the United States today is being raised in a female-headed household with welfare as its principal means of support. One child in twenty will spend over ten years in the welfare system. Children in such welfare-dependent families will grow up with little or no experience of a working adult parent. As a consequence, they will have little conception of working for self-support as adults. One way of breaking this cycle is to restore the work ethic to welfare families by requiring parents to work to receive benefits. Welfare should be based on mutual obligations between welfare recipients and society, not on one-way handouts.

Requiring able-bodied welfare recipients to work will reduce welfare dependence and promote self-sufficiency. At present less than 3 percent of adult AFDC recipients are required to participate in workfare or training programs in any given month. The federal government should require states to raise participation in such programs incrementally to 50 percent. The key to ending welfare dependency is to establish full-time work requirements, which are continued as long as an individual remains on welfare. But federal law restricts states' authority in requiring work; most states are permitted only to require welfare recipients to work on a part-time or temporary basis. Such federal restrictions on workfare should be eliminated.

Plank 97. Enforce financial responsibilities of parents.

There are five million fathers in the U.S. today who pay little or nothing toward the support of their children; the financial support burden is left to the mothers alone or to the taxpayer. The current legal system makes it difficult for mothers to collect delinquent child support payments. Child support award levels are extremely low, and less than half the number of absent fathers pay the full amount awarded. Penalties against a father who does not pay are minimal.

The child care enforcement system must be reformed. Court-awarded child support payments should be set as a fixed percentage of the male parent's income. Because fathers frequently default in paying court-ordered child support awards, the child support payment should be enforced by automatically garnishing the father's salary unless both parents agree otherwise. Thorough reform of America's child support payment system could raise the income of female-headed families by as much as $10 billion annually.

— CONFRONTING THE — POVERTY INDUSTRY

Plank 98. Use vouchers to empower welfare recipients and reduce dependency on the "poverty industry."

When poor people are told where to live, where to send their children to school, and who must provide them with social services, three things happen. First, the poor are made to feel that they are incapable of deciding anything for themselves or of advancing on their own. Second, potential self-help efforts to provide services are undercut by outside professionals. And third, an industry of professional service providers, construction and housing management firms, and school teachers have self-interest in maintaining the poor in a state of dependency.

Welfare dependency will never be cut until this industry is broken up. One effective way of doing this is to shift away from the policy of providing services by funding providers to a policy of vouchers. These would give the poor the financial means, through certificates earmarked for certain services, to become regular purchasers of such services as housing, education, and day care. In this way the poverty industry will become dependent on its clients, rather than the reverse. The poor will acquire a sense of independence and control, the first step on the road from poverty.

Plank 99. Reduce restrictions on community organizations providing services to the poor.

Some of the most effective initiatives in dealing with poverty come from within poor neighborhoods. Public housing tenants have scored major successes in tackling social problems, for example, (see Plank 111), and neighborhood groups have provided innovative and economical services such as day care and employment counseling. Yet a plethora of licensing and other regulations established under pressure from professional service providers often make it impossible for effective but uncredentialed local groups to compete with the well-established poverty industry in providing services to the poor.

Plank 100. Reduce welfare benefits to individuals with income above the poverty line; where appropriate, provide a corresponding income tax deduction to offset the reduction in welfare benefits.

Federal, state, and local governments currently spend over $150 billion per year in means-tested welfare benefits. This amount equals nearly $5,000 for every poor person in the U.S. Over half of welfare funds go to persons who are not poor even before they receive welfare benefits. Many persons receiving welfare benefits also pay federal income tax.

Federal welfare benefits to persons above the poverty level should be reduced. Reductions in taxation should replace welfare payments as a means of raising the standard of living of these low-income persons. Welfare benefits to all taxpaying recipients, moreover, should be reduced, with the reduction offset by a corresponding reduction in tax rates for these individuals.

Plank 101. Give states the option to tailor Aid to Families with Dependent Children payment levels.

High AFDC payment levels encourage welfare dependency. Reducing welfare benefits will reduce welfare dependency dramatically. However, uniform welfare benefit reductions are not always advisable. States should be given the option of paying lower levels of benefits to families where prolonged welfare dependency has become a problem or to families that are capable of self-support. Such a policy of targeted benefit reductions would promote self-sufficiency in a practical and humane manner.

Currently, federal law restricts the ability of states to modify benefit levels for different types of AFDC families. Each state pays the same level of benefit per child to all families within the state. States should be allowed to pay lower benefits to families with no children under the age of six. These families are clearly more capable of self-support than are families with children who are not yet in school.

231

States should be given the authority to pay lower welfare benefits to families that exhibit long-term welfare dependence. For example, a state may wish to adopt a system of graduated benefits, which are reduced the longer a family remains on welfare: a family in its first year on welfare would receive higher benefits than a family that had been on the welfare rolls for four years, the second family would receive higher benefits than a family that had been on welfare for ten years, and so forth. Such a policy would distinguish between families in need of short-term help and those that have become permanent wards of the state.

STRATEGY

Welfare's purpose is to help the poor, not to benefit middle class social service providers. Welfare for able-bodied Americans should not be a way of life, but a temporary helping hand. In return for assistance, therefore, the poor have the responsibility to use that help to improve their situation. A welfare system that is decentralized, allowing states and the poor themselves to try to find answers to problems, is *more likely than any centralized, bureaucratic system to find answers to poverty.*

Efforts by Congress to reform the welfare system, unfortunately, always seem to end up with little real change but a much larger price tag. Even liberals admit that there are many problems with the existing system, but they have been no more successful than conservatives in breaking through the opposition to change.

OBSTACLES

It may seem strange that, although Americans across the political spectrum call increasingly for fundamental reform of the welfare system, real reform always seems to be frustrated. The reason for this is that welfare reform, as all reform, threatens powerful groups and institutions benefiting from the existing system. They thus lobby to frustrate action that would help the poor but hurt the bureaucrats and others in the welfare system. Among those blocking welfare reform are dogmatic liberals who cannot bring themselves to accept that big government programs have failed to conquer poverty. Another, even more powerful group comprises welfare administrators and professional service providers who see their empires and paychecks threatened by such ideas as decentralization, vouchers, and self-help. And third, there are many private sector groups, from retailers who gain business from the food stamp program to construction firms that build public housing, who lobby hard to preserve and expand federal welfare programs. The result is that genuine welfare reformers invariably face a solid phalanx of opponents who claim to speak for the poor but are primarily interested in protecting their own dogmas and pocketbooks.

TACTICS

Challenge the "Compassionists." *Conservatives should challenge those who mouth support for the poor but offer as a "fix" government programs that perpetuate dependency and hopelessness among the poor. Conservatives should take the offensive by attacking the motives of those resisting reform, pointing out how the welfare industry lobby talks about the poor while it pockets most anti-poverty spending itself. Supporters of the poor should mount legal challenges to licensing codes and other restrictions on self-help.*

Mobilize the Poor Against Their Exploiters. *Conservatives need to work with community leaders, who recognize the deficiencies of the current system, to build political opposition to those who oppose real reform. In particular, conservatives should work to highlight successful local efforts to address dependency and poverty, and demand changes in the law to permit such examples to multiply.*

Spotlight the Poverty Industry. *Public attention should be focused on the poverty industry that exploits and denigrates* *the poor. Conferences on the poverty industry should be organized and hearings should be held in Congress to identify the composition of the industry and investigate its behavior. Abuses should be publicized in the way that Pentagon spending on toilet seats and coffee pots has been reported.*

Provide a Clear Alternative. *Reform is only possible if Americans believe that conservatives offer an alternative to current welfare policies. The current system should be attacked, but conservatives must emphasize they want a welfare system that works.*

COALITION FOR VICTORY

State and Local Officials. *State and local officials will benefit from flexible federal assistance policies that encourage innovative solutions to particular local needs. Decentralization empowers state and local governments at the expense of central government. Getting rid of federal red tape, therefore, is very popular at lower levels of government.*

Taxpayers. *Though they want to help genuinely poor families, taxpayers feel they do not get their money's worth from today's welfare system. Thus calls for a more effective and economical system should have wide appeal, as would a workfare proposal and a plan to tighten up on parental responsibilities. And even in richer states which would face cutbacks in federal support, appeals to the common sense of* *targeting help where it is needed most should win taxpayer support.*

The Poor. *The poor have most to gain from welfare reform. The choice and dignity provided by vouchers and local control would appeal to the majority of poor Americans who sincerely want to get out of poverty. Tougher parental requirements and workfare would appeal to the working poor, who resent the free ride given to those on welfare. And the challenge to the poverty industry would strengthen the position of neighborhood-based organizations.*

Chapter Fourteen

Reducing the Uncertainties of Retirement

Elderly Americans understandably fear any talk of "tampering" with Social Security. And for good reason. Many are almost totally dependent on the federal social insurance programs for their livelihood during retirement. Moreover, because the Social Security system is open to manipulation by politicians, there is always the chance that deficit reduction efforts, or other political pressures, will interrupt expected benefits. Thus even reasonable reforms of the system, intended to improve its soundness, meet with resistance from the elderly.

America's elderly will continue to fear for the security of their pensions until there is a change in policy to achieve two objectives. First, the Social Security system must be made more resistant to political interference, banishing fears that benefits will be cut or delayed. But second, and in the long run more important, steps must be taken to diversify the sources of pension income for the elderly, so that Americans are not excessively dependent upon Social Security. In particular, Individual Retirement Accounts should be allowed to play a greater role, and other private pension plans should be encouraged.

Plank 102.   Guarantee Social Security Benefits.

The Supreme Court has ruled that the elderly have no contractual right to their promised Social Security benefits, despite the payment of past taxes into the program.   Congress has the authority to reduce Social Security benefits, or cut them off altogether, for any of the elderly at any time. This leaves the elderly in constant fear that they will lose some or all of the benefits on which they have come to rely for their basic livelihood. Congress can and should improve the legal protection for Social Security benefits. It should guarantee that these benefits cannot be cut after retirement.

Social Security benefits should be guaranteed by providing that at the time a worker retires he or she would receive a U.S. government bond stating his or her contractual right to those benefits. All individuals already retired would receive such a bond as well. The bond would not change the amount of the retiree's promised benefits. It would simply be a contract with the government promising that the retiree will receive his monthly benefit amount each month for the rest of this life, plus cost-of-living-adjustment (COLA) increases.

This guarantee would provide retirees with the same legal status for their Social Security as U.S. Treasury bondholders have for their government bonds. Congress no longer would have the legal authority to reduce or cut off Social Security benefits.

Plank 103. Require an annual Social Security "statement of account."

For most American workers, Social Security is the largest investment they will ever make. This year, the maximum total payroll tax, including employer and employee shares, is $6,759 for an individual worker. In two years, this will climb to $7,600. Despite this enormous investment, few working Americans have any idea of the status of their Social Security account.

To remedy this, each worker should receive an annual "Statement of Account". The statement should report: 1) the total amount of payroll taxes paid by the worker and his or her employer each year over his or her career; 2) that these funds are not held by the government in a separate account for the worker, and have themselves earned no particular amount of interest; 3) the expected annual retirement benefits in present dollars that Social Security will pay the worker assuming continued annual earnings at the same relative level; 4) the amount of annual survivor's or disability benefits currently payable on the account and the length of time for which such benefits are payable; 5) significant limitations on benefits, such as the loss of benefits for outside earnings above certain levels; and 6) whether the program's Trust Funds are projected to be able to pay those benefits under optimistic, intermediate, and pessimistic assumptions, as listed each year in the annual reports of the Social Security Board of Trustees.

These Statements of Account should not add to the bureaucracy of the Social Security Administration. To avoid this, and maintain complete objectivity, the responsibility for developing and mailing the reports should be contracted out by the Secretary of the Treasury to an independent accounting firm.

240

—— DEVELOP PRIVATE —— ALTERNATIVES

Plank 104. Create a "Super IRA."

Of all government programs, Social Security has the most widely recognized and broadly utilized private sector alternatives. Pensions, IRAs, Keoghs, 401(k) plans, and other savings vehicles perform the same functions as Social Security retirement benefits. Private life insurance performs the same function as Social Security survivors' benefits for workers under age 65. Private disability insurance performs the same function as the program's disability benefits. Private health insurance can perform the same function as Medicare.

For today's young workers, the benefits paid by Social Security will not be a good deal in return for the huge investment paid into the program. Even if all promised benefits are paid, they will represent an effective interest rate on the huge payments into the fund over workers' careers of close to zero, or below zero for many. Blacks and other minorities who are younger on average than the rest of the population will receive an even worse deal under the program.

241

Chapter Fourteen

Social Security has been a good deal for today's retirees, and their benefits should not be cut now or in the future. But the system needs to be modernized and liberalized for today's young workers. These workers should be given the freedom to choose to rely more on the private sector and less on Social Security for their future retirement and insurance needs. The vehicle for this could be a "Super IRA" option. This option would allow workers to use an expanded IRA system to substitute private retirement, survivors, disability, and medical benefits for their Social Security benefits, to the extent they chose. With such an option, workers would be given an opportunity for improved benefits and a good deal in their retirement, while strengthening Social Security for the elderly of today and tomorrow. Unnecessary government dependency and spending also could be reduced sharply as a result.

Plank 105. Foster private pensions and enhance their transferability.

Millions of Americans enjoy private pensions supplementing their Social Security income. More than half of current workers are covered by pensions. These pensions are essential to the U.S. retirement system, and federal policy should focus on maintaining and expanding them. The 1986 tax reform legislation, however, placed substantial restrictions on many pension alternatives. For example, the annual maximum contribution to a 401(k) plan, which allows accumulation of savings contributions for retirement, was slashed from $30,000 to $7,000. Withdrawal restrictions further limited the viability of this attractive pension alternative.

These restrictions should be relaxed and maximum contribution limits restored. These pensions not only add to the ability of workers to provide for retirement through the private sector, avoiding reliance on government, they also add to national savings.

The pension system also can be enhanced by making pension contributions and rights more portable from one job to the next. This can be accomplished simply through greater reliance on defined contribution plans, where the employer and the employee contribute to an account which goes with the employee from job to job. Such plans also avoid any problem of underfunding or company insolvency undermining pension benefits, since the worker has control of the funds to support his retirement in his own account. Federal policy should encourage greater reliance on such defined contribution plans, which are better suited to the modern mobile work force.

Plank 106. Reduce payroll tax rates.

On January 1, 1988, payroll tax rates climbed again. Another automatic increase is scheduled for 1990. These 1988 and 1990 increases alone will raise payroll taxes by $25 billion per year to start. The payroll tax already constitutes an enormous burden on employment, destroying jobs and limiting economic opportunity. The continual increases in payroll tax rates since 1977 have outweighed reductions in income taxes for lower income workers, leaving them with higher tax rates overall. For younger workers, the payroll tax burden is now so high that even if they received all Social Security benefits now offered, those benefits would represent a bad deal.

The latest annual report of the Social Security Board of Trustees shows that full Social Security benefits can be paid for the next 25 years even without the 1988 and 1990 payroll tax increases. Indeed, these tax increases can undermine the economy sufficiently to create financial difficulties for Social Security in the near term.

The 1988 and 1990 payroll tax increases consequently should be repealed. To avoid increases in payroll taxes to finance Social Security benefits when the baby boom generation retires, efforts should begin now to slowly increase reliance on private sector alternatives and reduce reliance on Social Security.

❋   ❋   ❋

STRATEGY

T*he solution to the economic uncertainties of retirement is to guarantee Social Security benefits to current recipients while expanding the opportunities for future retirees to participate in private alternatives. The American retirement system needs to be modernized so that today's younger workers will have greater freedom to choose among the broad range of private alternatives for their retirement and insurance needs, rather than being forced to rely so heavily and unnecessarily on the government. The public broadly supports the payment of promised benefits to the elderly. But Americans are not blindly wedded to the current systems and institutions for providing for retirement. They recognize major problems with the status quo and are open to suggestions of better ways to provide for future benefits.*

OBSTACLES

The most significant obstacle to achieving reform is the tremendous politicization of retirement issues, particularly Social Security. Indeed, the election campaign trail is littered with the bones of politicians who dared to mention reform. The politicization of retirement issues focuses on the fear of the elderly that they may lose their benefits. Clever politicians have turned this fear into votes by painting reformists as villains who would reduce Grandma's Social Security check.

Another obstacle is that retirement seems very distant for young people. Consequently, motivating them to support reform is difficult, even though ultimately they have the most to win. Many others who might support fundamental reform need to be convinced that it is politically feasible before they will expend any resources or effort.

TACTICS

Redefine the Debate. *The dynamics of the Social Security debate must be changed. First, Social Security benefits must be guaranteed as discussed in Plank 102. This will make it impossible for political opportunists to exploit the fears of the elderly and lay the foundation for reform. Second, younger workers must be given the opportunity to increase* *reliance on private retirement funds. This will ensure a secure and prosperous retirement for future generations.*

Highlight the Broad Problems. *The status quo will not serve America's young well. The problem is not just the huge financial difficulties Social Security will face when the baby boom generation retires. Payroll taxes are now so high for today's young workers that even if they received the benefits currently promised, the program would be a bad deal for them. These workers are forced to invest so much more in the system than prior generations that they are precluded from choosing private alternatives. High payroll taxes and the lack of savings produced by the public system threaten prosperity and opportunity for young people today. These problems need to be highlighted.*

Form a Compact Between the Generations. *The current dynamics of the Social Security debate seem to pit the generations against each other. The elderly rightfully demand what they perceive to be a fair return on their life-long investment while younger workers view the pay-as-you-go system with suspicion, wondering if it will be solvent when they retire. Reforms should be presented as a new compact between the generations. Today's elderly will receive their benefits in full, but fundamental change is needed to allow today's young people to have security in their retirement as well.*

247

Confront the Fairness Issue. *Retirement issues are fairness issues with conservatives clearly offering the fair and compassionate solutions that liberals do not. It would be unfair for current beneficiaries or future beneficiaries who have paid into the system to lose their benefits or have them reduced. Similarly, it would be unfair to require future generations to pay higher portions of their incomes to support other beneficiaries simply because of a demographic phenomenon. Conservative solutions eliminate this unfairness by guaranteeing benefits and creating more attractive alternatives.*

Highlight the British Model. *The popular appeal and efficiency of a private alternative to Social Security is found in the British experience. In 1968 a private retirement program was created to parallel the government program. Later, British workers were given the right to switch to the private system. The response was dramatic; nearly 50 percent did so. The success of the British model should be documented and publicized in the U.S.*

Build Public Support for a Constitutional Bond. *Public support should be mobilized for constitutional bonds to guarantee benefits. A bill should be introduced in Congress this year calling for such a bond guarantee. Groups and individuals which represent the elderly — especially those that have fought Social Security cuts in the past — should back this effort.*

Make "Statement of Account" a Top Priority. *Plank 103 urges that each worker receive an annual statement of account which reports the total amount he or she has paid into Social Security over the years, as well as other important information. Making this a high-profile priority will raise public awareness of the need for reform in a way that does not elicit fears of benefit cuts. A full and fair disclosure bill should be introduced in Congress as soon as possible.*

COALITION FOR VICTORY

The Elderly. *Current Social Security beneficiaries number about 37 million, including close to 30 million retirees. These retirees will benefit from a constitutional bond guaranteeing their benefits. In return for such a guarantee, the elderly should support privatization efforts that will improve prospects for younger generations. Numerous opinion polls show the elderly are concerned about the legacy they will leave the young.*

Today's Workers. *Workers of all ages will benefit from private alternatives to Social Security such as the Super IRAs discussed in Plank 104. Without such alternatives, these workers could face sharply reduced retirement income from Social Security. Even if their full benefits are paid, they will receive a bad deal from the system in return for their huge*

249

tax payments and will have lost the freedom to choose among the broad range of superior private alternatives.

Post Baby-Boom Workers. *The generation now entering the workforce and those who will enter it in the next decade are much smaller in number than the baby-boom generation preceding them. When the baby-boom generation retires, this smaller generation of workers will have to supply the contributions to fund the benefits of the aged baby-boom generation. Without changes in the current system, this will require increases of 50 to 75 percent in Social Security taxes. A system of private alternatives will make such onerous tax increases unnecessary, while ensuring retirement income for both generations.*

Blacks and Other Minorities. *Because of their youth on average and lower life expectancy, blacks and other minorities receive a particularly bad deal from Social Security. They have much to gain from fundamental reform that would allow them to participate in private alternatives that would not penalize them for fewer expected retirement years. Unlike Social Security, private retirement plans can be structured so that recipients with lower life expectancy collect larger payments in the early years of retirement. Under a private plan, moreover, when an individual dies before receiving all of his or her benefits, those benefits can be passed to survivors.*

250

Labor. *Organized labor should support reform that will improve retirement prospects for its workers, offer them more freedom of choice and a better deal and avoid sharply increased payroll taxes in the future. Unions can develop private alternatives under their auspices, helping workers to manage and invest retirement funds and develop insurance protection, which would build more worker loyalty to the union organization. British labor supported private sector options to Social Security in Great Britain for precisely this reason.*

Business. *Business should support fundamental reform to avoid massive future payroll tax increases. The financial industry, which will help invest and manage private retirement funds and administer private insurance programs, should especially support fundamental reform which allows greater reliance on private options.*

Chapter Fifteen

Creating an Opportunity Society

All Americans should be able to pursue the American dream. Yet many minority Americans have been encouraged to believe that they are incapable of reaching for that dream, because they cannot acquire the skills, education, or capital to be successful. However, opportunities are not created by special preferential government programs or relaxed educational and workplace standards. These lead not to the American dream, but to the nightmare of quotas, reverse discrimination, and abject dependency on government.

Creating opportunity for all Americans means removing those barriers that hurt everyone, but are particularly onerous to the poor and minorities. This requires action in three areas. First, the poor should have the same choices in education that are considered a right by mid-

253

dle-class Americans. That means education vouchers and the tearing down of barriers to private schools in the inner city. Second, there needs to be a national effort to rid the inner cities of the scourge of crime. And third, steps should be taken to enable the poor and minorities to draw on their strengths in establishing businesses and acquiring their own homes.

—— Education ——

Plank 107. Make education vouchers available for low income Americans.

Public schools have failed the very Americans who need them most — the poor. These Americans cannot move easily to neighborhoods with better schools or take their children away from bad public schools and pay private school fees. Instead they are a captive market, forced to accept the worst that their local public school offers.

Vouchers are certificates of a given value which can be used instead of cash to purchase services. The provider of services is paid with a voucher and then turns in the voucher to the government for cash. Eduction vouchers would give low income parents the consumer clout they need to demand better education. Making public schools dependent on these vouchers for at least part of their finance, and allowing parents to use the vouchers at private as well as public schools, would force teachers and school administrators to shape up quickly or face a loss of students and money. In addition, in many inner city neighborhoods, there are very effective community based private schools, catering for the poor but struggling financially against the public school monopoly. Vouchers would strengthen such schools, providing poor Americans with a real alternative.

Plank 108. Reduce regulatory impediments to private schools serving low income families.

Hundreds of inner city private schools have sprouted across America, providing an alternative and excellent system of education for poor and usually minority Americans. They have high standards, and they are financed by modest fees and support from the neighborhood. The fact that poor parents are prepared to find money to send their children to such schools is testimony to their quality. Building codes, teacher certification requirements and similar government regulations, however, threaten many of these alternative schools.

255

These regulations should be streamlined to establish quality, not certification, as the test for a school. In particular, federal grants to help fund schooling, such as Title 1 assistance for disadvantaged children, should include a mandate requiring local jurisdictions to remove or streamline licensing and other restrictions which place unreasonable restrictions on private institutions seeking to provide education to low-income Americans. In addition, the Federal Trade Commission should investigate school and teacher licensing requirements to determine the extent to which they inhibit competition, and issue recommendations for appropriate legislation or federal regulation.

—— Crime ——

Plank 109. Increase law enforcement in the inner-city.

Blacks are almost twice as likely as whites to be raped, robbed or suffer an aggravated assault. Each year, more black Americans are killed in criminal violence than the number of black servicemen killed during the twelve years of the Vietnam War. Besides the personal tragedy of this criminal violence, crime forecloses the chances for economic revival in many of America's inner-cities. Entrepreneurs in crime dominated areas often cannot sufficiently maintain the safety of their own property or employees to enable their businesses to continue to function efficiently.

States and local governments must devote more law enforcement resources to combating crime in the inner city. Increased police manpower and patrols are required. Officials must target and crack down on neighborhoods that are especially vulnerable to burglaries, robberies, muggings, drug dealing, and prostitution. More authority, as well as political and moral support, needs to be given to the black law enforcement chiefs and executives who serve black minority communities.

These steps may require increased funding. But law enforcement is the primary purpose of government, and where crime becomes rampant, government is not doing its job.

Plank 110. Adopt a crime victims' Bill of Rights.

For too long, the U.S. legal system seems to have been concerned only with the rights of those accused of crime.

257

The rights of innocent victims have been ignored. State and local governments can remedy this by adopting a crime victims' Bill of Rights in their jurisdictions. Such a measure could provide for the right of the victim to present evidence at trial through his or her attorney showing the guilt of the accused, including testimony from the victim. Once guilt has been determined and the sentence is being considered, the victim should have the right to make a statement on the impact of the crime to the judge or jury who will decide the sentences. The concern of the victim should also be weighed in considering plea bargains.

Most important, the victim should have the right to restitution from the criminal to compensate for the harm caused by the crime. Where the criminal has no resources to pay such a restitution award, the criminal should be required to work while in prison, with most or all of the earnings going to satisfy such restitution requirements. If necessary for full restitution, the criminal's earnings could be garnished after release from prison until the victim is completely compensated.

Plank 111. Support neighborhood crime prevention programs.

Residents in U.S. inner cities are ready to fight back against crime. Their efforts can be marshalled through neighborhood crime prevention programs. Such programs would organize inner-city residents to create crime watch patrols. Such patrols of neighborhood residents would take turns patrolling their neighborhood on a scheduled basis, particularly at night. They would look for any suggestion of criminal activity and immediately report suspicious activity to the local police. A communication system would be established so that the patrols could relay information immediately to police officers expecting patrol reports. Such patrols have already been successful in reducing crime in many inner-city neighborhoods and public housing projects. Local governments should take the lead in organizing and assisting crime watch patrols. The Department of Housing and Urban Development should require Public Housing Authorities to support development of such patrols as well.

— Economic Development —

Plank 112. Encourage municipalities to contract with neighborhood groups to provide municipal services.

A basic requirement for economic growth in a neighborhood is good services. If garbage is not collected, streets regularly patrolled, and sidewalks maintained, it is difficult to entice businesses into the area. Yet poor neighborhoods tend to be at the bottom of the priority scale when it comes to services. And so a spiral of poverty continues as low tax revenues yield poor services and poor services mean no new businesses to raise the tax base.

To break this spiral, the city should contract with neighborhood groups for services. These groups have a greater interest than outsiders in delivering good services.

Tenant organizations have proved excellent managers of public housing in several cities. Neighborhood groups have provided day care services, garbage collection, street maintenance, juvenile rehabilitation programs, and other services. The federal government could encourage states and cities to make greater use of such neighborhood-based services by linking existing grants to states and cities to greater use of such alternative providers.

Plank 113. Reduce barriers to minority businesses rather than making them dependent on set-aside programs.

With the best of intentions, the U.S. has tried to foster business creation among minorities by giving such businesses special preferences — called set-asides — for federal contracts. This strategy has failed. For one thing, it reinforces the idea among minorities that they can succeed only by handicapping other Americans. For another, it has led to corruption, with many non-minorities using a minority "owner" as a front to obtain federal contracts. Worst of all, the bureaucratic set-aside programs usually suffocate genuine entrepreneurship.

The way to foster minority enterprise is to remove barriers to enterprise and to encourage minority firms to pursue their market advantages. Barriers to minority enterprises include local zoning and home work restrictions, which often prevent poor entrepreneurs from opening businesses in their own neighborhoods; minimum wage laws and the Davis-Bacon Act, which make it difficult for employers to recruit low skilled minority workers; and local building code and occupational licens-

261

ing restrictions, which make it hard for entrepreneurs to launch businesses.

The Federal Trade Commission, in cooperation with the federal Small Business Administration and various small business and minority organizations, such as the National Federation of Small Business and the Council for a Black Economic Agenda, should review and identify federal, state, and local regulations that hamper minority business creation. The FTC then should issue recommendations for reform to state and local governments, taking action itself in the case of federal impediments and in those cases where non-federal regulations conflict with established federal statutes to promote competition.

STRATEGY

Conservatives *believe that America is a land of opportunities for all, regardless of race, color, or creed. Conservatives also recognize that certain groups can be prevented from pursuing the American Dream by government barriers and policies.*

*Within the black community there is increasing accep-
tance that government programs have not led to general improvement. The relative success of Asian Americans in
prospering without special assistance and the successes of
black neighborhood self-help community organizations
within black neighborhoods make the idea of reducing barriers, rather than giving government "help," seem far more
plausible to most Americans.*

OBSTACLES

*Resisting change is the leadership of the black community,
which prefers to fight the battles of the 1960s. There are also
organizations, individuals, administrators, and private-sector firms which benefit considerably from programs which
reward some minority Americans, while erecting barriers
against most. For instance, some public school teachers do
not wish to see parents having choice in the education of their
children; housing management firms do not wish to see poor
Americans managing their own housing projects; and elites
who benefit from affirmative action do not want to see opportunities opened up for all.*

TACTICS

Support the Public Housing Privatization Movement.
*The success in winning 1987 congressional approval of
legislation to permit public housing tenants to manage, and*

ultimately to own, their homes should be a case study of how an opportunity society agenda can succeed. Conservatives worked with inner-city minority public housing residents who wanted to improve the condition of their projects. They identified housing agencies, unions, and patronizing liberals as the barriers to effective self help, and fashioned legislation to foster the goals of tenants. Liberals and special interest groups who opposed that legislation then found themselves in a bruising and embarrassing fight with the poor and decided to concede.

Promote Choice and Community-Based Services. *Low-income minority parents and inner-city private schools can be mobilized into a political force for education vouchers which will be difficult for the education establishment to resist. Conservatives also need to build alliances with neighborhood organizations denied the chance to provide services to their own communities. And they need to work with small business organizations to identify and publicize barriers to minority entrepreneurship. Conservatives need to unmask those who claim to support the poor and minorities while actually denying them access to the mainstream. In addition, conservative legal organizations, copying the tactics of liberal "public interest" law groups, should use legal action creatively to confront those who oppose reform.*

Attack Crime. *America's poor are the number one victims of crime. Perhaps nothing prevents the poor from taking ad-*

vantage of new opportunities more than crime. Crime is the primary disincentive to business locating in poor districts and it robs the poor of the few resources they have. Clamping down on crime must be a feature of any anti-poverty program. Conservatives should insist that crime is discussed in any debate on poverty.

COALITION FOR VICTORY

New Black Leaders. *One reason it has been so difficult for conservatives to win the support of black Americans is that the conservative message has been distorted or opposed by the official black leadership. Although most black Americans actually share basically conservative views on crime, education, and self-help, this official leadership continues to denounce these ideas and to urge black Americans to turn to government for their advancement. Yet increasingly, new black leaders committed to conservative ideas are challenging the dominance of the old-style leadership. These new leaders are open to conservative ideas and policies and could be powerful allies in gaining the political support of black Americans.*

Neighborhood Organizations. *Many organizations in the black community have grown frustrated at the ineffectiveness of government programs and angry at the paternalist attitude of government officials. These organizations have great confidence in the abilities of ordinary black Americans,*

265

and strongly support the ideas of self-help and choice. It is these organizations that invariably are the catalysts for improvements in poor communities. Self-help resident organizations in public housing, for instance, have successfully attacked drug use, the high school drop-out problem, and juvenile crime. Black churches have taken the lead in organizing housing rehabilitation and job training. Conservative Opportunity policies would help such organizations directly by enhancing their role. And conservatives have already discovered, in the case of the campaign for public housing privatization, both that such groups are enthusiastic about cooperating with them and that the groups make potent political allies.

Mainstream Americans. *Almost every American supports the goal of helping the poor and providing opportunities for minority Americans. Most Americans are not liberals by nature, yet they tend to support liberal policies, for two reasons. First, mainstream Americans hear the liberal rhetoric about wanting to help minorities and the poor, and assume that the policies that go with the rhetoric actually will achieve the goals. And second, they rarely see conservatives working directly with the poor and minorities and so tend to be skeptical about the motives of conservatives. Thus the strategy outlined above would undercut the policies and position of current liberal leaders and demonstrate to average Americans that minority citizens support conservative ideas.*

Heritage Foundation Contributors

Stuart M. Butler, Director of Domestic Policy Studies.

John E. Buttarazzi, Policy Analyst.

Milton R. Copulos, Visiting Fellow in Energy Studies.

Peter J. Ferrara, John M. Olin Distinguished Fellow in Political Economy.

Eileen M. Gardner, M.J. Murdock Fellow for Education Policy Studies.

James L. Gattuso, McKenna Senior Policy Analyst in Regulatory Affairs.

Edmund F. Haislmaier, Policy Analyst.

Edward L. Hudgins, Walker Senior Policy Analyst in Economics and Director of the Center for International Economic Growth.

Stephen Moore, Grover M. Hermann Fellow in Federal Budgetary Affairs.

William Peterson, 1987 Visiting Scholar in Labor Economics.

Robert Rector, Policy Analyst.

Melanie S. Tammen, Research Associate, Center for International Economic Growth.